Collins

Student Workbook

CAMBRIDGE
IGCSE® ENGLISH
AS A SECOND LANGUAGE

Mike Gould, Jane Gould and Lorna Pepper

Suitable for Cambridge IGCSE® English as a Second Language syllabuses 0510 and 0511

Contents

Section 3: Writing for a purpose

Section 4: Listening

1 Finding and selecting information

Understanding charts and tables

As you have seen in your work from the Student Book, information can be organised and presented in a range of ways, such as through **charts**, **tables** and text.

For example, Maniche talks about a survey of favourite sports activities done by his classmates.

> *Out of my class of 25, ten said soccer was their favourite activity; six preferred table-tennis, seven stated that basketball was best, but just two preferred handball.*

1 Can you complete the pie chart below, based on what Maniche said?

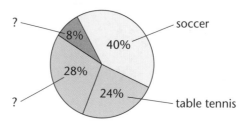

2 This chart presents another survey of a different class's favourite sports.

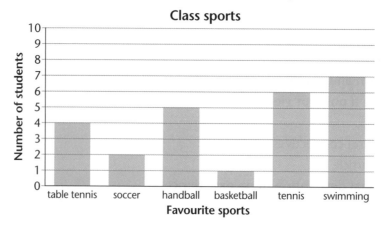

a) How many students liked soccer best? ....

b) What other five sports were mentioned by students?

....

....

c) Which sport was preferred by 28% of the class? ....

d) Which was the **least** favourite sport? ....

e) Which was the **most** popular sport? ....

Top tip

Use **superlatives** and **comparatives** to make sense of information, for example, when comparing or contrasting data and measurements. Comparatives are words or phrases such as *higher than…* or *lower than*, which compare more than one thing. Superlatives describe the highest/most or lowest/least of something, for example, 'most popular book, highest mountain.' For more practice in using comparatives and superlatives see pages 41 and 58.

Understanding graphs and diagrams

In an exam you are likely to have a question that includes text with a **graph** or **diagram**. Read the text below.

Luca's sports goal

Luca was delighted when he was given the job of making sport more popular in his school. He had always loved sport, ever since he was five years old when his older sister used to throw him a tennis ball in their back yard. Learning how to catch a ball gave him confidence, and he realised that by practising you could improve at anything. Now, he is captain of the school soccer team. But, when his teacher showed him the graph below, he knew he needed to act.

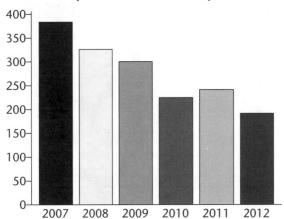

School students who participate regularly in sport (at least once a week)

Luca knew he had a big task on his hands. 'The numbers don't lie,' he says. 'Not enough students are doing sport and it's getting worse all the time. We need to find out why.' For this reason, he has asked all students who do not do sport regularly to fill in a questionnaire. The results are surprising. They show that it is not that students do not want to do sport. In fact, 80% of those questioned said they would love to do more sport, but money, opportunity and **peer pressure** were all given as reasons why they do not.

1 Which of this information is given in the graph, and which is given in the text? Circle the correct answer.

Reasons why students are not doing sport	*graph*	*text*
Numbers of students not doing sport in 2010	*graph*	*text*
When Luca first began to like sport	*graph*	*text*

2 Which of these statements is *true* about the information in the graph, which is *false* and which is *not given*? Circle the correct answer.

The biggest drop in students doing sport was between 2009 and 2010.	*true*	*false*	*not given*
Student participation in sport has fallen every year.	*true*	*false*	*not given*
Students do not do as much sport now because of the cost, what their friends think, and lack of opportunities.	*true*	*false*	*not given*

1 Finding and selecting information

Skimming and scanning: understanding headings

Subheadings on websites or in information books and leaflets, describe in a word or two the main information in that section.

Imagine you have found this website about teenage activity holidays in Spain. You want to find out more, so you click on 'Basketball camp' and see this menu of subheadings. By clicking on these, you would be able to find out more detail on that specific topic.

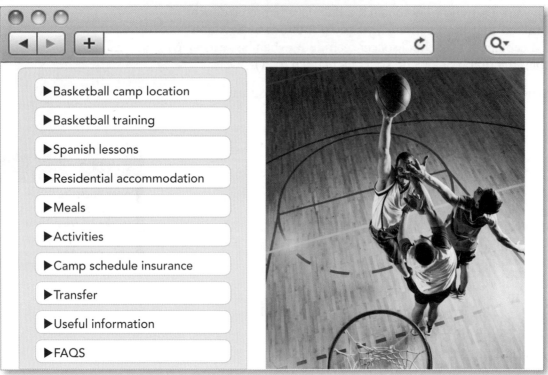

▶Basketball camp location

▶Basketball training

▶Spanish lessons

▶Residential accommodation

▶Meals

▶Activities

▶Camp schedule insurance

▶Transfer

▶Useful information

▶FAQS

1 Which heading will you click to find answers to the following questions?

a) Where is the camp based? .....Basketball camp location...

b) How can you improve your knowledge of Spanish?...

c) What sort of food will be provided? ....

d) What are the sleeping arrangements like? ....

e) Are there facilities for disabled people?...

Using skimming and scanning to find information

Imagine you want to find out more detail about the activity holiday.

2 **Skim-read** the text on page 7 and use the subheadings to decide which paragraph you will read to find the answers to these questions. Just write down the number of the subheading.

a) How many people will there be in a Spanish class? ....

b) What kind of room will I stay in? ....

c) When does the two-week course take place? ....

d) What other activities are there besides basketball and Spanish lessons? ....

e) What language is used for the basketball lessons? ....

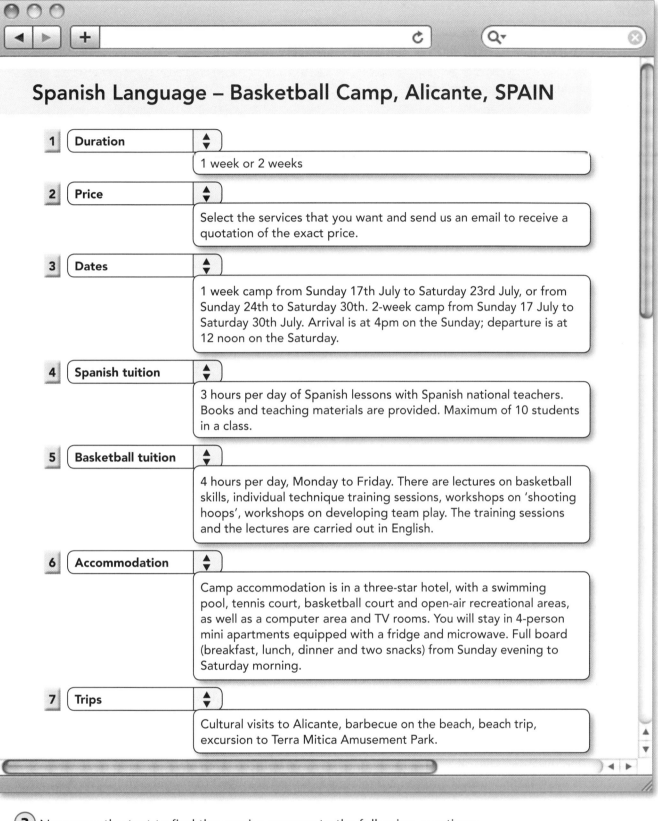

Spanish Language – Basketball Camp, Alicante, SPAIN

1 Duration

1 week or 2 weeks

2 Price

Select the services that you want and send us an email to receive a quotation of the exact price.

3 Dates

1 week camp from Sunday 17th July to Saturday 23rd July, or from Sunday 24th to Saturday 30th. 2-week camp from Sunday 17 July to Saturday 30th July. Arrival is at 4pm on the Sunday; departure is at 12 noon on the Saturday.

4 Spanish tuition

3 hours per day of Spanish lessons with Spanish national teachers. Books and teaching materials are provided. Maximum of 10 students in a class.

5 Basketball tuition

4 hours per day, Monday to Friday. There are lectures on basketball skills, individual technique training sessions, workshops on 'shooting hoops', workshops on developing team play. The training sessions and the lectures are carried out in English.

6 Accommodation

Camp accommodation is in a three-star hotel, with a swimming pool, tennis court, basketball court and open-air recreational areas, as well as a computer area and TV rooms. You will stay in 4-person mini apartments equipped with a fridge and microwave. Full board (breakfast, lunch, dinner and two snacks) from Sunday evening to Saturday morning.

7 Trips

Cultural visits to Alicante, barbecue on the beach, beach trip, excursion to Terra Mitica Amusement Park.

3 Now **scan** the text to find the precise answers to the following questions:

a) How many people will there be in a Spanish class? ....

b) What kind of room will I stay in? ....

c) When does the two-week course take place? ....

d) What other activities are there besides basketball and Spanish lessons?

....

e) What language is used for the basketball lessons? ....

1 Finding and selecting information

Finding information, answering efficiently

Look again at the web page on page 7.

1 Write down five questions you could ask someone else – they should have single-word or short phrase answers. Use the question prompts below.

What ....?

When ....?

How ....?

Where will ....?

How many..?

Going further

In order to make the most of the time you have in your reading and writing exams, keep your answers brief. For example, look at this question and answers by two different students:

> What kitchen equipment is provided for the holidaymakers?
>
> Adriana: *The four-person mini apartments are all equipped with a fridge and microwave.*
>
> Karl: *A fridge and microwave.*

Clearly, Karl's answer will take less time to write but still contains all the necessary information.

2 Here are some details about a holiday itinerary from another website. Read the text and then answer the three questions that follow as efficiently as you can. Answer in single words or short phrases. Do not include any unnecessary information.

> **Diving students – Days 1 and 2.** ⬍
>
> We arrive on the island by boat very early Monday morning at 7am, when your scuba diving instructor James will talk to you about some key safety information. He has been an instructor for ten years, so he knows what he's talking about! Then, at 10am, it's into the pool for our first practice session with all the gear. This session is vital because it is when you'll learn about breathing and entering the water. By 12 o'clock you'll be finished and ready for hot tea and snacks. Then, after a good night's sleep, it's back again at 7am on Tuesday for session number 2 in the pool. This time, we'll be testing how well you can swim in your diving gear, which isn't as easy as it sounds. If you can complete ten lengths, you're strong enough for the sea.

a) What day and time do students arrive? ....

b) Who will talk to the students?...

c) Why is the first session vital?...

d) What time will the session finish?..

e) When will they begin session number 2?...

f) How will the instructors know if the students are strong enough swimmers for the sea?

....

Identifying facts and opinions

In your reading and writing exams, you may be asked to pick out **facts** or to recognise an **opinion**, or to pick out facts supporting an opinion. Are you clear what each of these are?

1 Which of these are facts, which are opinions? Circle the correct choice.

People use mobile phones too much.	*fact*	*opinion*
There are thirty students in our class.	*fact*	*opinion*
I received a text message at 5pm on Saturday.	*fact*	*opinion*
Speaking face-to-face is pointless; text messages are much more efficient.	*fact*	*opinion*

> **Glossary**
>
> **fact** – something you can prove beyond any reasonable doubt
>
> **opinion** – a personal point of view which others could disagree with

Facts used in arguments

2 Facts can be used to make a point effectively or persuasively. Which *one* of these three facts would you choose if writing an article about how *good* mobile phones are? Tick your answer.

Fact 1: 60% of all people questioned thought mobile phones were a good thing.

Fact 2: I questioned five friends. Three said they thought mobile phones were a good thing.

Fact 3: 40% of people questioned were against mobile phones.

3 Now write one sentence explaining your choice.

I chose Fact .... *because* ....

> **TG CD-Rom**
>
> Worksheet 2

Going further

4 Read this short paragraph about mobile phones:

> It is absolutely clear that mobile phones are popular with just about everyone. You cannot argue with the facts, such as 60% of all people questioned being in favour of them. Ask anyone, and they will tell you all the wonderful things mobile phones can do. It is obviously true that they are an essential part of modern life.

How does the writer show the strength of his or her viewpoint here?

a) Underline any strong **adverbs** (words ending in *-ly* that give more emphasis, e.g. *totally*).

b) Circle **imperative verbs** (verbs that give commands or instructions, e.g. *Look … Take …*).

5 Now write **two** sentences giving your own strong opinion about something. Choose from one of these topics, or one of your own:
- Cruelty to animals
- How much top sports or film stars are paid
- The way some people behave towards disabled people

Your first sentence should begin with a strong adverb.

Your second should use an imperative verb – perhaps to do with what actions must be taken. Use this prompt if you wish:

It is totally/completely/utterly/absolutely .... *that* ....

....

....

Going further

Emotive words are particularly powerful words that clearly show a writer's or speaker's attitude or strength of feeling.

The same situation can be written or spoken about in very different ways. Read this letter to a local newspaper:

> I am writing to complain about what happened yesterday afternoon. A mob of students shattered the peaceful atmosphere of our beautiful town yesterday afternoon. Their aim, they said, was to protest to the local council about the proposed closure of the town's library. Well, I thought they had a strange way of going about it. I saw twenty young men and women, screaming and stabbing the air with their posters, marching down our high street. They demanded to see the leader of the Town Council and hand over a petition. It is absolutely clear, in my view, that this disgraceful event should never have been allowed to take place. I make this plea to the town authorities: act immediately to prevent such a thing happening. And get these thugs to face up to what they have done.
>
> **Mrs I. M. Cross**

1 Write down the facts of what happened. There should be no emotion in your facts. You could complete the sentences started below.

Yesterday, a group of ....

This took place in ....

The students wanted to ....

2 Now, decide which sentence in the letter directly describes what the writer's viewpoint of the march is. Write it here.

....

....

3 Underline the key emotive words in the letter which show the writer's *opinion* of the students (for example, *mob*).

4 Select any further words or phrases that show the certainty of the writer's viewpoint and are used to make the argument more powerful. Write your choices below.

a) Find strong adverbs:

adverb 1: ....

adverb 2: ....

b) Find imperative verbs that express what should be done:

verb 1: ....

verb 2: ....

Emotive language

Words and phrases can be 'loaded' in negative or positive ways, as you have seen in the newspaper letter: for example, a *group/mob/gang*. Remember this when reading, and also when writing to argue your own point of view.

(1) Look at the letter on page 10 again. Choose one word or phrase to sum up the writer's attitude to the students and their demonstration.

....

(2) Here are three headlines for a report about the march. Decide which:

- shows the students in the worst light (most negatively)
- shows them in the best light (most positively)
- is reasonably balanced (neutral).

Circle either negative, positive or neutral below.

STUDENT MOB SHATTER TOWN'S PEACE	*negative*	*positive*	*neutral*
LIBRARY'S SUPPORTERS MAKE POINT PEACEFULLY	*negative*	*positive*	*neutral*
STUDENTS MARCH IN PROTEST AGAINST LIBRARY CHANGE	*negative*	*positive*	*neutral*

(3) One of the students on the march read the letter on page 10. Here is her response. Circle the word in each case which presents her feelings *most strongly and accurately*.

I am writing to protest about the <u>fantastic/dreadful/thoughtful</u> letter sent in by Mrs Cross.

Our march through the town was <u>violent/passionate/lively</u> because we believe it is <u>fairly/totally/a little bit</u> wrong of the council to close our <u>wonderful/dreadful/dull</u> library.

For the writer to say we were 'screaming' is a complete exaggeration. We <u>pleaded for/asked/demanded</u> a meeting with the council leader, but he would not listen.

Going further

You will have to argue your point of view on occasions.

(4) Now write a final paragraph for the student's letter, saying what you want to happen next. Make what you say sound emotive and strong. Try to:

- use the most powerful **nouns** (like 'mob') or **adjectives** (such as 'passionate') you can think of
- include an **imperative verb** to show what should be done
- include powerful **adverbs** to go with adjectives ('*totally* clear', '*completely* true,')

Write your paragraph here:

Finally, I would like to ....

....

....

....

Close reading for detail

Read the following paragraphs from a magazine article about a special horse race in Mongolia, called the 'Mongol Derby', and then answer the questions below.

Time yourself: How long does it take you to do question 1? If you can complete it in under four minutes you are doing well. Reread the text to check your answers and see how accurate you were.

Riders prepare for Mongol Derby:

toughest horse race in the world

The race

This summer, riders from around the world will have their first chance ever to tackle the Mongol Derby, a 1000 kilometre long horse race through the harsh Mongolian landscape. It is being billed as the 'biggest, most dangerous equine affair on the planet'.

The riders

Twelve of the 26 riders taking part are British, while other competitors come from Mongolia, Australia, South Africa and Spain. 'We had about 100 applications and selected just 26,' said a spokesman.

One British rider, Katy Willings, was attracted to the extreme physical challenge. 'To have the chance to experience one of the last truly nomadic cultures – riding across a true wilderness – made the whole thing irresistible,' she explained.

(1) Answer the following questions:

a) How far do the riders have to travel during the course of the race?

....

b) How many riders are going to take part in the Mongol Derby?

....

c) Name **two** countries which will be represented by riders in the Mongol Derby.

.... and ....

d) Which country does Katy Willings come from?

....

Now read this longer version of the text about the Mongolian horse race. Then answer the next set of questions. Be accurate this time, rather than fast.

Riders prepare for Mongol Derby:
toughest horse race in the world

The race
This summer, riders from around the world will have their first chance ever to tackle the Mongol Derby, a 1000 kilometre long horse race through the harsh Mongolian landscape. It is being billed as the 'biggest, most dangerous equine affair on the planet'.

The riders
Twelve of the 26 riders taking part are British, while other competitors come from Mongolia, Australia, South Africa and Spain. 'We had about 100 applications and selected just 26,' said a spokesman.

One British rider, Katy Willings, was attracted to the extreme physical challenge. 'To have the chance to experience one of the last truly nomadic cultures – riding across a true wilderness – made the whole thing irresistible,' she explained.

How the race started
The idea of the race was thought up about four years ago. 'Because the horse is sacred in Mongolia we decided to organise a horse race,' said an organiser. 'It is based on Genghis Khan's ancient postal system – where riders crossed Mongolia to Eastern Europe in about 14 days, changing horses every 40km along the way. It's a massive challenge.'

What happens in the race
The race starts on 22 August at the ancient capital of the Mongol empire, Kharkhorin. The riders will swap horses every 40km and more than 700 semi-wild Mongolian horses will be used during the race.

Each competitor is given a race-map with the locations of each changing station, but they are essentially on their own. Throughout the race riders will stay with nomadic families, sleeping in tents, eating mutton and drinking the traditional fermented mare's milk.

'The Mongol Derby is a real test of the rider's skill and endurance,' say the organisers. 'This will be no ordinary horse race – it's not just a test of the horse's speed.'

How long it will last
The closing ceremony is planned for 5 September, but because this is the first race of its kind, organisers do not know how long riders will take. 'We're allowing two weeks for the slowest riders, but are expecting the fastest ones to complete in about five days – it just depends whether the riders are in for the race or for the cultural experience and adventure,' said the spokesman. 'And also, of course, they have paid quite a lot of money to take part.' The race costs $4450 (£2800) to enter and competitors must raise a further $1600 for an organisation which supports rural communities in Mongolia.

(2) Answer the following questions in the spaces provided.

a) How many people applied to take part in the Mongol Derby?

....

b) Why did Katy Willings want to take part in the horse race? Give **two** reasons.

Reason 1: ....

....

Reason 2: ....

....

c) How long did it take Genghis Khan's horse riders to carry a message right across the Mongolian Empire?

....

d) With whom will the riders spend the nights during the race?

....

e) What aspects of traditional Mongolian life will the riders experience? Give **two** details.

....

....

f) What qualities does the Mongol Derby test in the competitors? Give **two** details.

....

....

The next two questions are slightly harder.

g) In what way is this horse race different from the usual kind of horse race?

....

....

h) Why might some riders not be in a great rush to finish the race, according to the organisers? Give **two** reasons.

Reason 1: ....

....

Reason 2: ....

....

Writing concise answers

Here is the last paragraph again from the last text about the Mongol horse race.

> ### How long it will last
> The closing ceremony is planned for 5 September, but because this is the first race of its kind, organisers do not know how long riders will take. 'We're allowing two weeks for the slowest riders, but are expecting the fastest ones to complete in about five days – it just depends whether the riders are in for the race or for the cultural experience and adventure,' said the spokesman. 'And also, of course, they have paid quite a lot of money to take part.' The race costs $4450 (£2800) to enter and competitors must raise a further $1600 for an organisation which supports rural communities in Mongolia.

1 Answer the questions below about this paragraph.

a) On which date will the prizes be given out?

....

b) Although they cannot be sure, about how long do the organisers expecting the race to last?

....

c) What **three** reasons are suggested for the riders taking part in the race?

....

....

....

> ### Top tip
> Remember, it is vital in timed exams to give the exact answer and nothing else.
>
> Now look again at your answers above. Could they be shorter and still answer the question?
>
> Imagine you had given this answer for a):
>
> **a)** *At the closing ceremony on 5 September, although they can't be sure when the race will end.*
>
> Cross out the words which are not needed and leave those that still answer the question 'When?'.

Identifying intentions

People's **intentions** (what they are going to do) can sometimes be hard to work out in texts. Look at this sentence:

*If I am given some money by my parents, **I might** go to Paris.*

The use of 'if' and 'might' means: it is *not certain* the writer will get money, and it is also uncertain, then, whether he or she will go to Paris.

(1) Now look at: ***When** I get some money from my parents, **I will** go to Paris. How* is this different from the version above? Select and then circle the correct meaning:

a) *It is likely/quite likely/not likely at all that he/she will be given money.*

b) *It is likely/quite likely/not likely at all that he/she will go to Paris.*

> **Top tip**
>
> Looking closely at the forms of verbs, and the use of words such as *might, may, could, should* (known as modals) can help you understand the intentions and future actions of people in texts. These modals can make a big difference to meaning.

Here, a student, Pavel, talks about his love of horses and things he has already done, will definitely be doing in the future, or would like to do (if possible):

Of course, when I go on holiday next year with my parents I'll be riding horses as we'll be staying at a ranch in Texas. I would love to take part in a trek across the mountains, but I can't do this until I've had more riding lessons. The ranch owners won't let me go on a proper trek in the mountains unless they are sure I know what I am doing. I could take some riding lessons here in Poland before I leave.

(2) Underline the modals and consider how they affect the meaning.

(3) Now, select and then circle true or false for each statement below. You will need to reread the text very carefully. The degree of certainty in what Pavel will do is shown by the modals used, such as *will, would, could.*

It is not very likely that Pavel is going to ride a horse on holiday.	*true*	*false*
Pavel is definitely going to ride a horse on holiday.	*true*	*false*
The place Pavel is going to stay at is a ranch.	*true*	*false*
Pavel is ready to do horse trekking.	*true*	*false*
It is impossible for Pavel to take riding lessons in his home country.	*true*	*false*

2 Inferring and implying

Understanding what is implied but not actually written

Images can bring lots of ideas into your mind even when no other information is given.

1 Find any **adjectives** in the word search below. For example, can you find 'alone'?

2 Then, shade in or list those words which you think could be used to describe the woman in the picture.

3 Finally, write here the two words you think best suit the picture:

Word 1: ....

Word 2: ....

H	O	P	E	F	U	L	X
D	Z	X	L	T	N	T	C
N	B	A	A	J	W	J	O
H	A	P	P	Y	E	S	L
I	L	O	N	E	L	Y	D
B	O	R	E	D	L	Z	U
R	N	B	I	T	T	E	R
P	E	A	C	E	F	U	L

When we **infer** something, we understand its meaning through the clues and details given. These suggest certain things, even if we are not told directly what is happening.

4 What can you infer about the person from the image? Complete these sentences.

I think she is .... because it appears that she is ....

It could be that .... and ....

Going further

5 Now imagine that the image on page 17 comes from an article in a newspaper. Here are three possible titles for the article. Under each one, make brief bullet point notes on what the article might be about. Then add a sentence saying why you think this.

ALONE AND UNWANTED

The article could be about:

- How society ignores ....

- Friendship and ....

I think this because ....

....

Memories Never Die

The article could be about:

....

....

I think this because ....

....

PEACE AND QUIET AT LAST

The article could be about:

....

....

I think this because ....

....

Understanding texts from clues

Here are the first few sentences of the article which goes with the photo on page 17.

ALONE AND UNWANTED

A free bus pass from the government is welcome when you are 60, but it is not what Dora Edwards really wants. At 75, a widow with arthritis, living in a high-rise flat, and with no children or grandchildren, what she yearns for most is someone … anyone … to talk to. Surely that's not too much to ask? The government says it is listening, but it needs to do more than just listen. 'Who is looking after my real needs?' Dora wants to know.

Glossary

yearn – desire or wish for something very strongly

1 You can work out the subject (the basic content of the article) by considering the clues. These are the words the writer has chosen – the vocabulary – and the factual information provided. Answer these questions about the article:

a) How old is Dora Edwards? ....

b) What free item does the government give you if you reach the age of 60? ....

c) Where does Dora live? ....

d) What does she suffer from? ....

e) What do you find out about her family? (Find **three** things.)

　1: ....

　2: ....

　3: ....

f) What does she want more than a free bus pass, according to the article?

　She would like ....

Going further

2 Now that you have understood the details of the extract, how would you describe the subject or main content of the article? You are not told directly: you have to work it out, to 'read between the lines' and infer.

Read carefully the five suggestions below. Then write A, B, C, D, E into the pyramid, putting the description that is closest to what the article is about at the TOP of the pyramid.

A: The things you can get for free when you are over the age of 60 in Britain.

B: The life of an old woman and what the government could do to make things better.

C: The importance of family.

D: Common illnesses suffered by the elderly.

E: Why high-rise flats are suitable for elderly people.

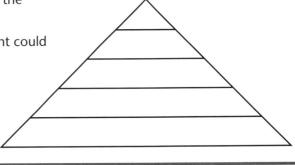

Inferring viewpoint

What an article is *about* and the **viewpoint** of the writer are slightly different things. For example, even if we know what the article on page 19 is about, the writer does not mention his/her view. So, how can we tell what they think?

1 Consider these choices made by the writer:

a) He/she uses the phrase *yearns for most* to describe Dora's needs. Is this a stronger or weaker phrase than: 'wants a bit' or 'would like'? Circle your answer below.

stronger   weaker

b) He/she uses a rhetorical question – one that does not expect an answer, or where the answer is obvious. Find this rhetorical question and write it below:

The rhetorical question used is..

2 Here, a student has written about the article. Based on your reading of the article, circle the words you think best describe the writer's viewpoint.

> The writer is clearly <u>concerned about/happy with/bored by</u> the situation facing older people, like Dora Edwards. He wants to make it clear that the government needs to <u>do more/do less/do nothing</u> to address the problem/issue/possibility of loneliness for the old. <u>It is vital that/It would be nice if/It would be quite good if</u> they acted rather than simply listened.

Here is the next part of the article. It contains another person's views.

> But, David Rimington, head of the local council for Dora Edward's town, takes a rather different view. 'We have offered Dora Edwards a regular visit from a social worker under a new scheme, "Call On Us", but I'm afraid she has not replied to our calls or letters. There is only so much we can do.'
>
> Dora admits that she is not keen to answer the phone, after getting nuisance calls last year from young people in the flats below, and that she often throws away letters she thinks may be junk mail. However, even if this is true, surely someone could have called round, rather than just phoned or sent a letter?

3 **a)** Now, consider the writer's viewpoint. What is David Rimington's view of the situation and how Dora has been treated? Tick the correct answer below:

A: The government has tried to do its best, but Dora has been difficult to contact. ☐

B: Dora is a nuisance and so the government should stop helping her. ☐

C: No one has helped Dora and he feels bad for her. ☐

b) Why has Dora not replied to the phone calls or letters offering her help? Give **two** reasons.

....

....

4 Choose one word to describe Dora's attitude to receiving messages from the outside world.

....

5 Choose one word to describe David's attitude to Dora. Explain your choices.

....

The power of imagery

You will not have to read imaginative stories in your reading exam. However, some of the techniques used by writers of such stories are also used in articles, letters and essays. For example:

- **clear** and **vivid vocabulary** to create a picture in the reader's mind
- the **use of imagery** (unusual or powerful comparisons) to make ideas come alive.

Read this extract from someone remembering a childhood experience:

> The forest was dark and I saw monsters in it, the swaying heads of sharp-fanged beasts, the pointed claws of primitive beings. The path snaked and twisted through the giant trees, and seemed to last an eternity. I ran, fleeing from my own imagination. I vowed never to read stories about old legends, and never to listen to Uncle's scary tales around the fire. But, all of this was too late. At that age, it wouldn't have mattered what I had read or seen or heard. The creatures who screamed and reached out to grab me from the army of branches were my own creations. If, indeed, they had jumped out, if they really had existed, I'm sure they would have been less awful in reality than in the murky depths of my mind where they were born.
>
> Years later, in my thirties, after having lived away for a long time, I revisited my village. I did that same walk through the forest. The path seemed straighter, the trees smaller, stubby and insignificant. What could have possibly made me feel so afraid back then?

1 Circle the words below that best describe the writer's state of mind as a girl.

relaxed   worried   anxious   terrified   confident   sad   angry   confused

2 What else can you work out about the girl's feelings from the imagery and vocabulary she uses?

a) When she says, *I saw monsters in it [the forest], the swaying heads of sharp-fanged beasts* what does she mean?

She means that the shapes of the forest looked like monsters in her mind and ....

....

b) What does *The path snaked and twisted* suggest about the path and how it looked?

It was ....

c) When the writer says, *I ran, fleeing from my own imagination,* what does this mean?

It means she was running away from ....

d) What does the metaphor, an *army of branches* suggest about the forest?

It suggests that the trees were ....

Going further

3 The last paragraph suggests that the writer has changed as she has got older. Find two things that appear to have changed about the forest.

....

....

3 Using information

Transferring information accurately

In your reading and writing exam you will need to transfer information accurately between the text you have read and the form or answers you are completing.

(1) Spot how many differences there are between the original correct text in column 1 and the student's answers in column 2. Then copy out correctly in column 4 . Make your capital letters really clear.

Original version	Student's answers	How many errors are there?	Your correct version
22 Hannover Terrace, London	22 Hanover Terrace, London	1 error	
Tariq Hassan Sulleiman is the School Principal	Tariq Hassan Sullieman is the School principle		
Tshwane is the African name for the Apies River as well as the name used for the Pretoria area.	Tishwane is the African name for the Apies river as well as the name used for the pretorai area		
My telephone number is 0788451990 and my email address is jjbrown@networkspeak.com	My telephone number is 0788415990 and my email adress is jjbrown@networkspeak.com		
Her job is Managing Director of Trucktrail Corporation	Her job is Managing Directer of Truck Trail Corporation		

(2) Here is a job advertisement. Can you transfer the correct information from the advertisement into the grid?

WANTED French and English speaking diving instructor for Pearl Diving Centre, Koh Tao, Thailand. Must be physically fit, an excellent swimmer, and have at least 5 years' experience as an instructor. Please call Mario Wilson, Centre Manager on 088699934 for further details.

The job	Where	Skills and experience needed	Who to contact, and what phone number

Top tip

Use black ink pen when you answer the questions, so your answers are definite and clear. If you make a mistake, draw one clean line through the wrong answer and write the correct answer above or next to it. Like this: ~~Adress~~ address

Key question words

1 Complete the following table, which shows some common key question words that you find on forms, and the kind of detail that you would need to look for.

Choose the correct answer for each gap from the box below the table.

Key question word on the form	The sort of detail to look for in the text
1 *Where exactly …?*	
2	A time. Remember to say am or pm, or to use the 24-hour clock – use the same format as in the text
3 *How much … cost?*	
4	Weight with a unit of measurement, e.g. kg or pounds or tonnes etc
5 *Age*	
6 *Address*	
7	First, middle and last names – as many names as you find in the text

> *At what time …* or *When …*
> A price with a unit of measurement, such as £ or $ or cents
> *How much … weigh?*
> A number in years, or years and months
> Number of a house/apartment, with a road and town
> *Full name*
> The name of a place, with some detail about it

Instruction words

2 Look at the box of numbers on the right, and then carefully follow the instructions below:

- **Circle** the highest number.
- **Tick** the lowest number.
- Put a **cross** by the number with two digits.
- **Underline** the answer to the sum 2 + 2.
- There are twelve numbers in the box.
  (**delete** as necessary):   *true   false*

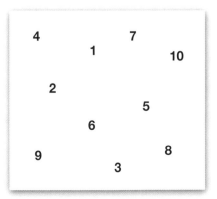

Handwriting

Handwriting is important in this exercise. All your letters should be clearly formed. Capital letters should all be bigger than lower-case letters.

1 Copy these sentences in your normal handwriting.

The quick brown fox jumps over the lazy dog.

....

Jim just quit and packed extra bags for Liz Owen.

....

William Jex quickly caught five dozen Republicans.

....

A large fawn jumped quickly over white zinc boxes.

....

Six big devils from Japan quickly forgot how to waltz.

....

Five or six big jet planes zoomed quickly by the tower.

....

These sentences are all called *pangrams*. You don't need to know this word, but can you guess what pangrams are?

2 Here are two handwritten responses to the same task. Go through each and circle any handwriting that is unclear or difficult to read and any grammatical mistakes such as missing or incorrect capital letters.

I have just started this wonderful new job in freetown. I am working in an Eco-friendly cafe making fruit smoothies for tourists. I love meeting new people; Yesterday a party of 20 Russian schoolgirls invaded us and we were so busy!

i have just started this wonderful new job in freetown. I am working in an eco-friendly cafe making fruit smoothies and tropical juices for Tourists. I love meeting new people; Yesterday a party of 20 Russian school-girls invade us and were So busy!

Changing from third person to first person

When you transfer information from a text to a form in the exam, you may have to change it from the **third person** (*he/she/name of person*) to **first person** (*I, me, we*).

1 Change these sentences from the third person to the first. An example has been done for you.

a) Dannii found the trip to the museum very boring. The curator spoke so slowly and she found herself yawning and rubbing her eyes. If only she could be at the swimming pool, she thought!

I found the trip to the museum very boring. The curator spoke so slowly and I found myself yawning and rubbing my eyes. If only I could be at the swimming pool, I thought!

b) Danni's friends were just as bored as she was. So, when the curator turned his attention to another school group, they all crept away to the cafe.

My friends ....

c) At the cafe, they all sat there, laughing and giggling. Then, to their shock, their teacher walked in and told them they had to leave.

At the cafe, we all..

d) Danni found herself and her friends back in the museum doing the same boring tour. The worst thing was, their teacher made them start the tour from the beginning again!

My Friends and I..

Subject and verb agreement

The changes above were relatively easy because you only had to change the **pronouns**, not the verbs. However, sometimes when transferring information you will need to go further. For example: *Dannii **hates** museums* (third person) becomes *I **hate** museums* (first person).

2 Change these examples so that the verb and **subject** (the one 'doing' the action) match correctly.

In the text it might say (in the third person)	You will write (in the first person)
Danni goes to school in Geelong	*I .... to school in Geelong.*
She loves doing athletics.	*I .... doing athletics.*
She is very happy to train.	*I .... very happy to train.*
She has completed three races.	*I .... three races.*
She has the same routine each morning .	*I .... the same routine each morning.*
She likes running by the sea by herself.	*I .... running by the sea by ....*

Finding information, transferring it to a form

Now read a bit more about Dannii and what she *does* like.

Dannii Tyler, 13, lives at 15, Kathy Freeman Avenue, Geelong, near Melbourne, Australia and has always loved the outdoor life. Perhaps that is because she was born on the opening day of the Sydney Olympic Games, 15th September 2000. Or perhaps because her road is named after the celebrated Australian athlete who won the 400 metres gold medal that year. She loves swimming, cycling and running so it is natural that the triathlon should be the event she would like to enter at a future Olympic Games.

As chance would have it, an inter-schools triathlon event came to Geelong, and Dannii was determined to take part, even though it was officially only open to those aged 14 or over. However, Dannii had already beaten lots of older students in swimming and running races at her school, Geelong High, and had taken part in two previous triathlons for younger students, so she decided to apply for the event.

Dannii was allowed to take part in the triathlon, and did very well, finishing 22nd out of 122 competitors, nearly all of whom were older than her. The triathlon was the Inter-School Gold Triathlon Event and took place on the weekend of the 15th–16th October. There were other triathlons taking place that month on the 7th to 8th and 23rd to 24th October, but they were outside her area so she didn't take part. Besides, one triathlon was enough!

Dannii rated her performance in the swimming as her best, as she came 18th out of all the competitors for that section. She finished 22nd for the cycling, which was ok, but she struggled a bit in the running, finishing much lower down the field. She realises that if she is to be a serious contender for future Olympic Games she will need to improve her speed and endurance in running in particular.

At the end of the triathlon, the Head of Athletics for the Geelong area, Sam Cawley, presented the winners with their medals, and then came and spoke to Dannii's parents, Michael and Arika. He told her how impressed he was with her performance, but suggested she now needed specialist training. He told her about the Elite Performance Group which trained every week on Geelong sea-front, and said being part of it would boost her chances of reaching national standards as she got older.

Dannii realises that if she wants to fulfil her dream of Olympic glory, she will need to join the Elite Performance Group.

Glossary

triathlon – a sports event when you have to swim, cycle and run all on the same day

contender – person trying to achieve or win something

elite – very special, only for a few people

1. Complete the form for Danii on page 27, including the personal details that are requested.

Application Form to join

ELITE PERFORMANCE GROUP, TRIATHLON, GEELONG

Section A

Full name of applicant:...

Age:...

Date of birth:...

Address:...

....

....

Name of parents:..

School attended:...

Number of triathlons completed:

1–2 ☐   3–4 ☐   5+ ☐

Section B

Which triathlon(s) did you take part in? [please tick]

8th–9th October ☐   15th–16th October ☐   22nd–23rd October ☐

How would you rate your performance in the three disciplines? [please circle]

Cycling: Good   Satisfactory   Poor

Swimming: Good   Satisfactory   Poor

Running: Good   Satisfactory   Poor

What do you need to work on most to improve your performance?

....

....

Section C

In the space below, write **one sentence** of between 12 and 20 words explaining how you found out about the Elite Performance Group **and** your reason for wanting to join it.

....

....

....

....

Making notes under headings

Read this local newspaper article. Afterwards, you are going to produce three lists of details under given headings.

1 Before you write anything:
- Skim read the article to get a general sense of how the information is organised.
- Read the three headings given on page 29 very carefully.
- Read the article more carefully. Take three different coloured pencils and underline the details relating to each heading in a different colour.
- Then write your lists – your notes – under the right headings.
- Remember that notes should not be full sentences.

'Be a friend' to your community

Have you ever thought what it is like to be alone, old and with no one to care for you? Unfortunately, there are many older people just like this in the town. So, I'm asking you, our readers, as the Editor of this paper, to help make things better. This will be our newspaper's campaign for 2013–2014.

Why are we doing it? It all started when we heard that the council had sent leaflets to everyone in the town, explaining that they would have to spend 20% more on employing carers to visit old people living alone. They said that people were just not doing enough to make sure that older neighbours and residents were looked after. The money for this care would mean that other services, such as recycling, would need to be cut.

It's not just the fact that not enough people are visiting older people or relatives to check that they are okay. As a newspaper, we had noticed for ourselves how the town is not very suitable for older people to visit. There are no benches to rest on in the main shopping street. The nearest public toilets are up a steep hill, and the only elevator in the main library is broken. In addition, the bus shelter is covered in graffiti and the timetable is in tiny print that no one, however young or old, could read.

So our paper wants to do something to improve matters. Join us and help. We intend to do two things. Firstly, we need volunteers to join our scheme to visit older people who can't get out of the house and would like some company just for a chat, or to do a few basic jobs. Secondly, we need young, fit and active readers to help us make the town more welcoming for older people. With the agreement of the council we have arranged for as many of our readers as are interested to help clean up the bus shelter, install benches and improve signs. To make sure everyone is involved, those who do not want to spend time cleaning or improving the town centre could make their first visit to some of the older people the council has told us about.

Please come and help. The more of us there are, the quicker we can get the jobs done, and the more people can be visited. Meet us outside the Market Coffee Shop at 10am. If you have any queries you can contact me, the Editor, Miles Smith here at the newspaper, or my Assistant Editor, Orla Martinez.

(2) Make your notes under each heading.

Who readers should contact if they are interested in helping

- ....
- ....

The problems the 'Be a friend' club has seen in the town

- ....
- ....
- ....
- ....
- ....

Actions that the club will carry out this weekend

- ....
- ....
- ....
- ....
- ....

Going further

Make notes below of details which show that the organisers are concerned for the wellbeing of the club members

- ....
- ....
- ....
- ....

Organising information, creating headings

Texts are often split into sections, with each section about a slightly different thing.

1 Here is a paragraph from an article about 'storm chasing'. Read it carefully.

Glossary

tornado – a violent, twisting column of air between the earth and sky

skyscape – wide view of the sky

barrage – powerful attack

A person who chases storms is, not surprisingly, known as a 'storm chaser', or even just a 'chaser', but their reasons for chasing storms vary. For many, their main intention is to witness a **tornado** at first hand, so actually getting up close to them and experiencing the fear and excitement is their key objective. However, others chase thunderstorms and get great pleasure simply because they enjoy seeing unusual or beautiful cloud structures and **skyscapes**, or want to watch a **barrage** of hail and lightning.

2 Which of the following headings best describes what this paragraph is about? Tick the best answer below. Be careful – do not find just one small thing in the heading that matches the paragraph. The best summary headings will cover the *overall* focus of the paragraph.

A: The dangers of storm chasing ☐

B: Why some people chase storms ☐

C: How lovely storms can be ☐

> **Top tip**
>
> **Information** and **explanation texts** tend to describe how and why things happen or people act as they do, so it is likely your headings and notes will do this too.

3 Read the paragraph again. Write down **three** reasons why people chase storms.

A: ....

B: ....

C: ....

Now read the remainder of the article about storm-chasing.

Storm chasers are not often paid for what they do, but it would be fair to say that they often provide valuable on-the-ground help for weather agencies and local government in the USA when storms are approaching. They upload photos or data from the equipment they carry with them, and this can help agencies predict the path of storms or confirm whether their own observations are correct or not. On the other hand, providing dramatic photos or footage of storms and tornadoes from the very spot where they are happening, can prove a money-spinner if television or news networks are willing to pay. Or they can be sold to picture agencies.

Storm chasing has probably been around for many years. Most people remember their first storm as a child and the excitement and fear it brought, and for some it becomes a career. Perhaps the first real storm chaser was a man called David Hoadley (1938–), who first chased North Dakota storms in 1956; he used data from local area weather offices and was the founder of *Storm Track* magazine. Another man, Neil B Ward (1914–1972) worked with the Oklahoma Highway Patrol to study storms, and made it possible for larger organisations to chase storms using detailed research.

Increasingly, storm chasing has entered popular culture, with perhaps the key event being the release and success of the film *Twister* in 1996. It was the second most successful film, financially, of 1996 in the US (the first being the box-office smash, *Independence Day* which was not about storm chasing, of course), suggesting a really strong interest in the subject. However, 'real' storm chasers complained that it gave a distorted and over-simplified view of the subject. This did not dampen the public's enthusiasm however, and the 2007–2011 series, 'Storm Chasers' on the Discovery Channel actually led to more people taking it up.

Nowadays, storm chasing is an increasingly sophisticated activity with participants learning about meteorology to help their quest, and using satellite-based tracking systems to pursue or predict the paths of storms. Digital video, digital SLR cameras and GPS phones have all made communication of data and images easier and quicker, but there are still many storm chasers who trust instinct and their own senses to be in the right – or wrong – place!

3 Using information

The first paragraph on page 31 continues the theme of 'why storm chasers chase storms', but it deals with two categories of storm chasers: those who do it for money and those who do not.

4 Make brief notes under these two headings:

Those who do not chase storms for money – how they are helpful

- ....
- ....

Those who chase storms to make money – how they make money

- ....
- ....

5 The first paragraph is mostly written in the **present tense** (*They upload photos …*).

a) What verb tense is mostly used in the second paragraph?

....

Give one example:

....

b) Are we told mostly about people, processes, or specific events?

....

c) What heading or title would you give to your set of notes for this paragraph as a result?

My title would be: ....

6 Now select three key points made in paragraph 2 about memories of storms and/or important storm chasers.

Point 1: ....

Point 2: ....

Point 3: ....

7 Finally, reread the last two paragraphs.

Here, a student has chosen a heading and key points for Paragraph 3.

> Paragraph 3 heading: US box-office smashes, 1996
> Point 1 : storm-chasing has entered popular culture with perhaps the key
> event being the release and success of the film 'Twister' in 1996.
> Point 2: 'Independence Day' was a box-office smash
> Point 3 the TV series, 'Twister' led to more storm-chasing by the public

a) What is wrong with these notes? Is the heading accurate?

It is a good/bad heading because ....

b) Is point 1 in note form? How could it be expressed more simply? Write a better version here:

Point 1: success of 'Twister' was ....

c) Is point 2 relevant or irrelevant?

It is relevant/irrelevant because the film 'Independence Day' is ....

d) Which part of point 3 is correct and which is incorrect? Cross out the wrong information, then write the correct information in its place:

The TV series, 'Twister' led to more storm-chasing by the public.

Now write the correct version:

The ....

8 Now write your own heading and notes for Paragraph 4 in the spaces below.

Paragraph 4 heading: ....

Point 1: ....

Point 2: ....

Point 3: ....

> **Top tip**
>
> Do not rewrite in full the points or sentences from the text. Leave out unnecessary words, for example, in the third paragraph, you would not need to include all the definite articles, and could put: *success of film, Twister, 1996* – no need for *the, in* and so on.

1 Sentences

What is a sentence?

Remember that a **sentence** begins with a capital letter, and ends with a full stop, question mark or exclamation mark. These punctuation marks help us understand what sentences can do.

Make a **statement**:	The crowd roared enthusiastically.
Ask a **question**, or make a request:	How does this machine work?
	Do you honestly expect us to believe that?
Give a **command** or **instruction**:	Turn right by the mosque.
Exclaim, to stress a point or show strength of feeling!	How awful that hat is!
	What a pity!

1 What sort of sentences are shown in a) to d) below? Write on the line the type of sentence shown. The first one has been done for you.

2 Then, for each question, tick what type of text it might have come from (such as a letter, a story or a diary).

a) *The music festival took place at the outdoor arena.* ...... **statement** ......

The line-up was great, with some of my favourite bands and singers performing. ......

Rihanna was fantastic! ......

What type of text?
email to a head teacher ☐   letter ☐   diary entry ☐

b) *What was that noise?* ......

He stopped for a moment and put his backpack down. Surely all the tigers had died out years ago? ......

Then he heard a growl and the sound of something crashing through the undergrowth. It was a tiger ......

What type of text?
email to a friend ☐   adventure story ☐   diary ☐

c) *Feed Timmo each morning.* ......

Put bins out for collection on Thursdays. ......

Water the plants on patio. Please don't forget to post that cheque! ......

What type of text?
mystery story ☐   newspaper report ☐   list left by parents while on holiday ☐

d) *What a day!* ......

I met my favourite pop star and got his autograph. ......

How cool is that? ......

What type of text?
diary entry ☐   information text ☐   newspaper report ☐

Types of sentence

Simple sentences

A **simple sentence** is usually short and contains a **subject** (the person who does the action of the verb) and a **verb** (a doing or being word), and can be useful for clear explanations and instructions. For example:

I [subject] *sat* [verb] *at the station.*

1 Add a **verb** to these simple sentences:

a) The atmosphere was amazing. She .... to the front row.

b) The crowd ....

c) Then, it all went quiet. The music ....

Compound sentences

A **compound sentence** can be used to balance ideas, or join two short or simple sentences of equal importance. You can use 'and', 'or' and 'but' to join the two sentences. For example:

*Our team played well **and** the players showed all their skills.*

2 Now write compound sentences about a meal you had recently.

a) The .... was tasty and the ....

b) My .... did the cooking, but .... did the ....

c) However, I prefer going out to eat really.

d) I am happy to go to .... or I like ....

Going further

Short sentences can be used in creative ways, too. Here, the short sentences suggest time is passing slowly (s = subject; v = verb).

s v   s   v   s   v
I sat at the station. The clock ticked. He wasn't coming.

3 Create three or four short simple sentences from this long sentence to make it seem tense or full of drama. You can add exclamation marks or question marks if you wish.

I waited by the door for my exam results to come and watched as people went past my window until I finally heard steps up the garden path.

Start with: **I waited by the door. Would my exam results ever** ....

....

4 Now write three or four short simple sentences to create tension in an exam or test situation. Start with:

Marcia sat in the exam hall. The ....

....

....

1 Sentences

Complex sentences

A longer **complex sentence** can add further information, provide contrast, show cause and effect, and so on. It can be made up of lots of parts, built around a main idea.

Let's take the exam room situation …

main part of sentence	extra 'bit' of information
You could hear a pin drop	*although the room was full of students.*

Usually the extra 'bit' does not make sense on its own, or sounds unfinished.

5 Draw lines to match the main and supporting parts of these sentences.

Although it was raining   *we couldn't get any tickets.*

Even though we queued for five hours   *we missed the last train home.*

Because we were forced to wait   *we managed to keep dry.*

6 Now, complete the following sentences, adding further information. You can base your ideas on a wasted trip to see a match and the journey home.

a) I arrived home .... although I managed to get a taxi.

b) My older brother said that .... even though he was sympathetic.

c) My mum kindly .... because I was so fed up.

In d) below, the main part and the extra part have been swapped around, for variety. Complete it in the same way.

d) While I realise that I should not have gone without tickets, I am determined to ....

....

7 In the following paragraphs:
- underline the compound sentence
- circle the complex sentence
- highlight the simple sentence/s.

a) *The market street was incredibly dark and there were suspicious figures lurking in the shadows. They seemed to be watching. Even though we were travelling light, we were dripping with sweat.*

b) *A neon light flickered. Because it was so late, all the hotels were shut. We walked up and down and we phoned all the hotel numbers. It was no good. Everything was closed.*

c) *Even though we were beginning to get worried, Alicia remained cool. She led us to the beach. There were lots of young people partying and there was plenty of space for us to sit. It was almost morning.*

Developing sentences with phrases

First of all, check your understanding of **nouns** (the names we give to things, people and ideas).

> Nouns can also be categorised as:
> - Common: *cat, dog, man, woman, dinner*
> - Proper: *Nairobi, Gandhi, Victorians, Ramadan, The Lord of the Rings*
> - Collective: *a **herd** of cattle, a **crowd** of people, a **team** of footballers*
> - Abstract: *hope, fear, loneliness, fatherhood*

Top tip

If some of the following are true of a word, it is likely to be a noun:
- it may follow the words/phrases *a, the, a few, some*
- it changes form to show singular, plural or possession, for example: *girl, girls, girl's, girls'*

1 Find the nouns in this pile of words and then sort them under the four headings below: common, proper, collective and abstract.

book   flock   tasty   believable   table-cloth
        lemonade   better   Cape Town   audience   tribe
motherhood   lunch   curiously   boredom
    engine   love   dull   gang   Walt Disney   lovely
cup   under   belief   Koreans   suspicion   Sydney   bored   Paris

Common	Proper	Collective	Abstract

Noun phrases are very important in writing because they allow you to pack a lot of information into a few words. The noun phrase has a noun as the **head word** (the part around which everything else grows). For example, in the following sentence the head word is the noun *soup*:

> *Enjoy my tasty, home-made soup, packed with the goodness of home-grown vegetables.*

The soup is *tasty*; it is *home-made*; it is *packed with the goodness of home-grown vegetables*.

Sentences such as this can contain more than one noun phrase. For example:

> *A nasty-looking, striped, buzzing insect* from *my overgrown garden,* landed on *my pale and exposed leg.*

2 Try building up the following sentences by adding noun phrases to them. Add **adjectives** and/or **nouns** in the spaces provided.

a) A beautiful, ... butterfly from the .... field near my house

   landed on our ....

b) That .... film we went to see was the best I have seen all year!

1 Sentences

Using pairs of words or phrases

You can also help readers understand your writing by using pairs of words to join sentences. For example, *either ... or*:

- *You could go home to collect the shirt. You could ask your brother to bring the shirt here.*
- ***Either** go home to collect the shirt, **or** ask your brother to bring it here.*

These joining words are called **connectives**.

1 Join the following pairs of simple sentences using the pairs of connectives in the box below.

> *Not only ... but also ...*   *Although ... nevertheless ...*
> *After ... then*   *If ... then ...*   *Either ... or*

a) You want to go. I will come with you.

....

b) I will wash my hair. I will go out to the shops.

....

c) We could have pizza at the Italian restaurant. We could have curry at home.

....

d) He is not very good at sports. He always does his very best at sports.

....

e) My friend enjoys playing volleyball. He enjoys taking part in competitions.

....

> ### Top tip
> Watch your use of commas! Try not to separate parts of a sentence with a comma when you need a connective or a new sentence. For example:
> - *We went to the show, I didn't enjoy it.* should be ...
> - *We went to the show but I didn't enjoy it.*

Going further

To develop your writing to a higher level you need to show that you can use a range of sentence types and lengths.

2 Take one of the sentences you made in task 1 and develop it into a paragraph. Write at least one simple sentence, one compound sentence and one complex sentence following the guidance on pages 35 and 36. Use the same topic to link them together into one paragraph.

More ways of joining sentences

Another way to join sentences is to use words ending in -ing. These are called **present participles**, for example, *singing*. They come from verbs but act like adjectives. Look at these examples.

Singing, the girl walked along the road. (Singing is describing 'the girl'.)

Giggling, the two friends made their way home.

Present participles can be joined with other words into phrases. For example, *singing a terrible love song*, or *giggling helplessly*. These phrases can be used in sentences:

Singing a terrible love song, the girl walked along the road.

Giggling helplessly, the two friends made their way home.

We can use these **participles** or **participle phrases**, to join ideas together. So,

The man was eating a biscuit. The man made a phone call.

can be joined together and written as:

Eating a biscuit, the man made a phone call.

> **Top tip**
> Note how, when the phrase is at the start of a sentence like this one, it is separated from the rest of it by a comma.

(1) Now use a participle or a participle phrase to join these pairs of sentences:

a) The dog growled. The dog gnawed its bone.

....

b) Hussain ran away from the fierce dog. Hussain tripped over a rock.

....

c) Frederich enjoyed every minute. Frederich danced along with the music.

....

d) Marina opened the window and looked out. Marina shouted out to her friends.

....

e) The snake hissed. The snake slithered in through the window.

....

f) The runner slowed down. The runner panted heavily.

....

g) Scott put his pen down and sighed. Scott left the exam room.

....

> **TG CD–Rom**
> Worksheet 3

1 Sentences

Going further

Here is an example of a slightly different participle phrase.

The water drained slowly from the swimming pool choked with old leaves.

This uses the **past participle** which ends in *-ed*, again to act more like an adjective. In this case, *choked with old leaves* describes the noun *swimming pool*.

Not only do participle phrases allow you to add information to your ideas, they also mean you can begin sentences in a variety of ways.

2 Can you add your own present or past participle phrases to these sentences?

a) The shopkeeper, ... at the counter, watched the woman carefully. (suggested verb: *stand*)

b) ...., the Cup was our first victory ever.
(suggested verb: *win*)

c) ...., they soon cleared up after the floods.
(suggested verb: *help*)

d) ...., she is popular all over the world.
(suggested verbs: *love, admire*)

e) ...., I thanked everyone at the party.
(suggested verb: *to be pleased*)

Using participle and noun phrases to build longer sentences and add detail is a really useful skill for making your writing clearer and more informative.

3 Describe your visit to a new shopping centre. Below is a basic outline of the writing. You can change and add to it using the skills you have learnt. Try to add something about:
- your excitement at seeing the centre for the first time
- which shops you visited – add details about one in particular
- what you thought about the shopping centre as a whole.

Remember to use a range of different sentence structures, and include some participle phrases and noun phrases.

I went to the new shopping centre yesterday. It was in the middle of town and ....

....

I couldn't decide which one to go into. Then I chose one and looked round it. It had ....

....

I thought they looked ....

....

Afterwards, I went ....

.... I left at 7pm.

Joining ideas to make more interesting sentences

Imagine you have these notes for a summary about Europe.

- London – capital city of England – population of over 7.5 million

You could write a compound sentence:

London is the capital of England and it has a population of over 7.5 million.

To make it more interesting, you could add variety to your sentence structures, for example, by using the word 'which':

London, which is the capital city of England, has a population of over 7.5 million.

Or by using brackets:

London (the capital of England) has a population of over 7.5 million.

(1) Now use the following notes to write a paragraph about one of the other capital cities of Europe. Choose a variety of sentence structures. Check that you have used punctuation correctly.

- Paris – capital city of France – population: 2.2 million people – River Seine flows through Paris
- Vienna – capital city of Austria – population: 1.9 million people – River Wien flows through Vienna

Your paragraph:

....

....

....

....

Going further

You could begin your paragraph about Paris by comparing it with London (in terms of size):

Smaller than London, Paris ....

(2) Try rewriting your paragraph from task 1 using comparatives

Your new paragraph:

....

....

....

....

For more on comparatives see pages 4 and 58.

1 Sentences

Using the active and the passive

Active and **passive** verb forms allow you to change the tone and effect of your sentences. They also add variety to your sentence structures.

Active: *I noticed the fire in the shop and I called the police* — The subject of the sentence is present and 'does' the action (noticing the fire/calling police)

Passive: *The fire was noticed and the police were called.* — The subject (the person who noticed the fire) is missing from the sentence, so the text seems more objective and 'distant'.

The passive style is especially useful for formal accounts which need a sense of authority, and where facts are more important than emotions.

1 Underline the use of any passive verb forms in the following text.

The shark was observed at 7am breaking the surface of the water approximately half a mile from the shore. Local coastguards were alerted and the shark was guided out to sea to safer areas before any harm was done to tourists.

2 **a)** Which of these forms of text do you think the text is most likely to come from?

    A: teenager's diary ☐

    B: encyclopedia entry for sharks ☐

    C: news report ☐

    D: police report ☐

b) In one sentence, explain why it would fit the form of text you have chosen:

    I think this style fits .... because ....

    ....

3 Finally, read this second version of the text written in the **active voice**.

I thought, 'wow' when I saw the shark at around seven this morning in the sea, I guess about half a mile or so out. Tourists were swimming right near it! So, I called the coastguards and they acted so quickly, and guided it out to sea before it could do any damage.

a) Underline the active verb forms in the text above.

b) Which of these forms of text do you think this text comes from?

    A: eye-witness interview ☐

    B: police report ☐

    C: poem ☐

    D: encyclopedia entry on a shark ☐

> **TG CD-Rom**
> Worksheet 4

2 Paragraphs

What is a paragraph?

A **paragraph** is a group of sentences usually about a single topic – the same main idea, theme, person or event.

Read this example:

> *Our school swimming pool needs repairing. There is no diving board, the tiles around the outside are covered in weeds and are broken, and there is a leak which means the water drains away quickly. The leak is probably at the deep end as you can always see muddy bubbles coming to the surface.*

1 What is this paragraph mainly about (what topic links all the points made)?

A: the missing diving board ☐

B: the leak ☐

C: the poor state of the swimming pool as a whole ☐

D: the tiles ☐

Topic sentences can help you structure paragraphs by acting as an introduction. For example:

Our school swimming pool needs repairing – you then go on to say what the problems are.

There are three steps to a healthier school – which you then name.

Please make time for these health requirements – you list what they are.

These in turn can help structure your whole essay.

2 A building company has sent an email to the school's headteacher about repairing the swimming pool. Unfortunately, a virus in the email has swapped the sentences around. Read it through carefully.

> **From:** Manager, Top Building Services
> **Subject:** Swimming pool repair
> **Date:** 8 October 2012 11:07:25 GMT+01.00
> **To:** Mr Iqbal, Aseef
>
> Dear Sir,
>
> Secondly, we will replace all tiles both on the bottom of the pool and around it. We will start by emptying the pool. Finally, we will return to fit the new diving board. As requested, here is our three-stage plan for repairing the school swimming pool,
>
> Yours,
> Mr I Brick, Manager

a) Which is the topic sentence in this email? Find the sentence which starts things off, and leads on to the others. Write it here:

....

b) Now write out the email in the correct order below:

Dear Sir,

....

....

....

2 Paragraphs

Linking ideas using connectives

When you link ideas, sentences or paragraphs, **connectives** can be very useful.

> Here are some of the main types of connectives:
> - Time order (chronological) and sequence: e.g. *at first, initially, later, then, next, finally*
> - Cause and effect, logical steps: e.g. *therefore, consequently, so that, as a result*
> - Development of ideas, or addition of new ideas: e.g. *also, in addition, moreover*
> - Contrasting ideas: e.g. *on the other hand, nevertheless, however, in contrast*

1 Join these ideas in or between sentences with a suitable connective, using the ones above, or similar ones:

a) The work by your company was very poor, and .... I am cancelling the contract.

b) The stream has completely dried up. .... the reservoir it leads into is 60% lower than last year.

c) Sam's speech went on for ages! ...., when it was over, we woke up!

d) There are many benefits to electric cars, for example economy. ...., they still cost a lot to buy.

e) I didn't like him; .... he didn't like me! ...., he still doesn't like me.

2 Can you spot the use of connectives in the paragraph below? Circle them and label them, T (time order), L (logical order/cause and effect), D, (development), C (contrast).

> *I am writing to report on the progress made on the new swimming pool.* (Firstly,) *the* ⎯ T
> *builders were late and so work did not begin until midday. Nevertheless, once there, they*
> *worked very hard indeed. As a result, the old tiles were removed rapidly. Moreover, they*
> *had drained the pool by sundown and told me work was complete for the day. Yet, when I*
> *went to look at the pool I noticed there were still some old tiles lying around on the grass.*
> *In the end, I called the manager and after a while someone came back to sort things out.*

3 Imagine you are one of the builders. You have to write an official explanation to your boss – the manager of Top Building Services – explaining why you were late. Here are some possible reasons:
- traffic
- oversleeping due to tiredness from work
- taking children to school
- an unforeseen event!

Use the connectives in the panel at the top of the page to help you recount what happened. You could start your email like this:

> Dear Mr Iqbal,
>
> First of all, I wish to apologise for my lateness to work yesterday.

Top tip

Adverbs, such as *fortunately* or *surprisingly*, can also help you 'signpost' your account of events in informative texts such as this.

Structuring paragraphs

1 Read these notes about Pelé, a famous footballer. They need to be turned into two paragraphs. Remember, a paragraph is usually about one main idea, or several linked ideas.

First, decide which notes fit which paragraph: Paragraph 1 = Pelé's background and early life; Paragraph 2 = Pelé's successes as a footballer and his life now. Write P1 or P2 next to each of the notes below.

Edson Arantes do Nascimento is a famous footballer.

He scored 1281 goals in 1363 games.

He was born in poverty.

He played with a sock stuffed with newspapers.

He is better known as Pele.

He is the top scorer of all time. ⟨P2⟩

He could not afford a football.

He became very wealthy.

He was born in Brazil. ⟨P1⟩

He is well known for supporting causes to help the social conditions of the poor.

He dedicated his 1000th goal to the poor children of Brazil.

2 Now that you have decided which points will be in your two paragraphs, turn the notes into sentences, which are joined together.

- You could use: *who, which, because, so, although, since, where, when* – or any other connectives.
- You could change the order of the ideas, or miss out words or phrases, or rephrase ideas.
- Try to have as much variety in your sentence structures as you can.
- Make sure you include a topic sentence.
- Check that you have written complete sentences. Each sentence must make proper sense and start with a capital letter and end with a full stop.

You could begin your paragraphs like this:

Paragraph 1 – *Pelé's early life was difficult …* (then write about his difficulties)

Paragraph 2 – *Despite this difficult start, Pelé went on to be successful.* (then write about his successes)

Notice the link between the first and second paragraph. The phrase *Despite this difficult start* refers back to the previous paragraph *and* leads the reader neatly onto the next stage.

> **Top tip**
>
> You could start Paragraphs 1 and 2 with other phrases, such as:
>
> *In his early life … In later life …*
>
> *As a child … When he was an adult …*

2 Paragraphs

Paragraphs with viewpoints and reasons

The best writing allows the reader to follow information or an argument clearly. Read this short opening paragraph to an article in a student magazine.

> I strongly believe that my parents should increase my pocket money. This would encourage me to work harder, and I wouldn't need to come to them every time I needed cash for the bus, to go to the cinema, or to meet my friends at the cafe. These friends, who all get more than I do in terms of pocket money, agree with my point of view. When we are chatting together, we all discuss how parents should really value their children. They are precious after all. So give them more!

1 Answer these questions:

a) What does the topic sentence tell us is the viewpoint of the writer?

It tells us that...

b) What does the definite article, 'this' refer to at the start of the second sentence?

....

c) Who are the 'who' referred to in 'who all get more than me …'?

....

d) Who does 'we' refer to in 'we all discuss …'?

....

e) Who does 'them' refer to in the last sentence?

....

Now read the following paragraph, which contains a viewpoint on a separate issue. Here, the writer starts with a general point and includes more and more detail to be persuasive.

> Our holiday on the island was wonderful for many reasons. Firstly, the — topic sentence
> weather was great, our room was comfortable and clean, and the hotel staff — builds on main idea, giving
> were very helpful. The young man on the desk even telephoned a local — further details why holiday was good
> jeweller when my wedding ring broke, and arranged for it to be repaired. — specific detail elaborates on one of the points in the second sentence

2 Answer these questions.

a) What is the viewpoint of the writer?

The writer's viewpoint is that ....

b) What three specific details are given in the second sentence about the holiday?

Detail 1:...

Detail 2:...

Detail 3:...

c) What even more specific detail, building on the second sentence, appears in the last sentence?

The specific detail mentioned is: ....

....

3 Now, have a go at adding more detail for yourself. Read the start of this account about a terrible holiday.

Our city break was dreadful for many reasons. For a start, the weather was foul, our room was dirty and small, and the hotel staff were rude and unhelpful.

a) Underline the three reasons in the second sentence why the city break was so bad.

b) Now choose one of the details from this second sentence and write a third, even more specific sentence, as in the example about the island holiday.

Write the final sentence here.

....

....

4 Imagine the above text comes from a letter to your sister or brother about your dreadful holiday. Plan two further paragraphs about other bad things from the holiday:

Paragraph 2 could be about your problems on arrival. Write down three possible problems:

A: Plane was late..

B: ....

C: ....

Paragraph 3 could be about your problems at the hotel. Write down three possible problems:

A: The swimming pool had no water in it, and ....

B: ....

C: ....

Use the images below to give you ideas.

5 Write the whole letter on a separate piece of paper. Use everything you have learnt about topic sentences, linking sentences, joining paragraphs and linking ideas.

2 Paragraphs

Linking opinions with evidence

When you argue a point of view, your paragraphs can build towards a powerful conclusion. You could begin with one argument, then add to it with new points. By the end you will have a case that no one could argue against!

Look at these arguments *for* an education system with no tests or exams:

A: Tests and exams make students anxious and worried.

B: Exams are boring; students could be doing fun stuff!

C: Tests and exams only measure a small range of skills.

D: Tests and exams waste teachers' time as they have to spend hours marking them.

1 Look at the examples below. They all provide evidence to support one of the points of view (A, B, C or D above). Circle the correct letter.

Our teacher, Mr Voronin, spent two nights marking our exams. This meant he didn't have time to prepare our lesson, so we just watched a video.	A	B	C	D
I never sleep well before exams.	A	B	C	D
Our Science exam was two hours long. There was no way it covered every scientific process in the world.	A	B	C	D
You don't see many students smiling and looking happy in exams. My friends often seem to be staring out of the window wishing they were somewhere else.	A	B	C	D

Connectives can be used to link the points and the evidence, where needed. You could use the following words and phrases to do this:

for example, such as, in this way, because, so, as a result.

Or sometimes: *which explains why ..., that accounts for ....*

Take this example:

Exams give you vital information about your progress. **For example,** ——————— point
after my maths exam, I could see clearly that I needed to practise using
percentages as that was the part of the exam I did least well in. ——————— evidence

2 Now, write your points here using a connective word or phrase. You can make one longer sentence or keep the sentences separate.

A: Tests and exams make students anxious and worried ....

B: ....

C: ....

D: ....

Going further

3 On a separate sheet of paper, write a short article of 100–150 words for a teenage magazine about the how exams make students feel. You can decide whether you want to focus more on the negative or positive feelings students have.

3 Vocabulary

Synonyms

A **synonym** can help you put other people's ideas into your own words. But, synonyms do not always have exactly the same meaning as one another. For example, there are many words in English which mean 'the place where people live', but each word has a slightly different meaning.

Glossary

synonym – a word which has the same or a similar meaning to another

Look at these synonyms for house:

slum   palace   bungalow   flat   residence   shack

Would you know when to use each of the above? Use a dictionary if necessary to find out.

1 Where would each of these people live? Find a word from the list above:
- a prince
- a very poor person in a city living close to many others
- an average person who lives on their own
- a very poor person living out of town
- an important official
- an older person who cannot climb stairs.

2 Here are some groups of synonyms. Write each set of words in order, from a mild feeling to the most powerful feeling. You can use a dictionary to help you. Sometimes the order will be a matter of opinion, not fact!

a) afraid   alarmed   nervous   panicky   terrified   scared   petrified

....

....

b) grief-stricken   sad   unhappy   miserable   depressed   distraught   tearful

....

....

c) happy   pleased   ecstatic   contented   delighted   positive   cheerful

....

....

3 Produce another list of synonyms connected with feelings (e.g. *worried, angry*) and order them from 'mild' to 'very strong'. You could type or write them in larger or darker font and print them out as a visual revision check.

3 Vocabulary

Going further

'Nice'

There is one nice little word in English which is really useful. And there are times when this little word is just the right word to use. But often this nice little word needs to be chopped out and replaced, because it is so overused it has lost any real meaning.

4 Read the following paragraph and underline all the uses of 'nice' in it.

My friend Luis is very nice to me. He and I had a nice time last Saturday when he took me to the nice burger bar in that nice shopping mall near us. It's really nice inside. Everything is nice and clean and it looks so nice and smart. And the food smells nice, too. And the taste! Well, the burgers we had looked nice and tasted nice. Luis paid for all we had, including an extra big nice milk shake. He really is nice.

5 Rewrite the paragraph, choosing words from the box to replace each 'nice' you have underlined. If you can think of different word instead, use it.

generous	fantastic	smart	well-designed	modern	fresh	up-to-date
delicious	appetising	scrumptious	kind	creamy		

....

....

....

....

'Say' and 'go'

'Say' and 'go' are two other words which we can often replace to express our ideas in a more exact and subtle way. The following exercise will help you use a wider vocabulary.

6 Read these sentences out loud. Then write which version tells you the most and suggests a story to you, and why.

A: 'It's my fault,' she said as she went out of the room.

B: 'It's my fault,' she whispered as she ran out of the room.

C: 'It's my fault,' she shouted as she staggered out of the room.

The version which gives the most information, and suggests a story is ....

because ....

7 Then write two more versions of the sentence which you might find in a story.

a) 'It's my fault,' she .... as she .... out of the room.

b) 'It's my fault,' she .... as she .... out of the room.

Using better vocabulary

It is important to learn and use a range of words connected to a particular subject or area. This can be helpful when you are writing a report or arguing a point of view on a particular topic.

1 Group the words or phrases in the box under the headings below. Are there any which go under more than one heading?

Building	Football	Cookery	Fashion
....	....	....	....
....	....	....	....
....	....	....	....
....	....	....	....
....	....	....	....
....	....	....	....
....	....	....	....

> design   architect   style   measure   trend   vintage   level   heat
>
> goalkeeper   simmer   door   line   makeup   accessory   elevator
>
> foundation   pot   red card

2 This poet has cleverly mixed vocabulary from cookery and football to create a poem.

    a) Underline the words or phrases to do with a cookery recipe in the poem.

    b) Circle any words which are just to do with football.

> *Take two rival teams*
>
> *And mix into a large stadium.*
>
> *Leave the crowd to simmer until kick-off,*
>
> *Then bring to the boil with an early goal.*
>
> *Allow to cool down after 45 minutes.*
>
> *Then, boil again until the cream comes to the top*
>
> *With a second goal after 10 minutes.*
>
> *Turn off after a further 35 minutes.*
>
> *Let the crowd stand for five minutes*
>
> *Before removing.*

Going further

3 Write your own six-line recipe poem about a journey to work on a crowded bus or train. Your poem could start with:

Take thousands of rushing people,

Press firmly into …

4 Here is the introduction again to the task on page 283 of the Student Book:

> There is a problem of too much traffic in your local town and the town council is considering setting up a 'congestion charge'. This means that anyone who wants to drive their car into the town centre will have to pay a sum of money to do so. You decide to write a letter to the council to give your views.

Read this first paragraph that a fellow student has written in response to this task:

Thank you for giving me the opportunity to speak to you at this public meeting. I feel <u>badly</u> that it would be <u>very bad</u> to set up a congestion charge for anyone driving a car into the town centre. It will be especially <u>bad</u> for the people who need the council's support the most. Many people won't be able to pay the charges. It will be very <u>bad</u> for people who live in <u>bad</u> areas, without buses or trains to get them into town. They need their cars to <u>get</u> themselves into the town centre. Shopping can be very heavy – how are they meant to <u>get</u> heavy things to the car parks on the outside of town? The elderly will be <u>very badly</u> affected. They can't be expected to walk all the way into town. The same goes for parents with heavy pushchairs and energetic young children. They need the cars to <u>get</u> into the centre as quickly as possible.

Replace each of the underlined words with one of the words below, to make the writing more varied and more precise. Write the letter (A to J) above each underlined word

A travel   **F** afford

B passionately   **G** iniquitous

C transfer   **H** unjust

D transport   **I** adversely

E remote   **J** unfair

You may need to check the meaning of some of the words in a dictionary.

4 Avoiding ambiguity

Types of prepositions

Prepositions are often short words or phrases that tell us how things relate to each other, or the position of things or people. For example:

- single-word prepositions – *at, over, near*
- two-word prepositions – *ahead of; instead of; near to*
- three-word prepositions: *by means of; in front in spite of.*

Prepositions often indicate:

- time – *at five o'clock; **after** the match*
- place (position) – ***on** the head; **in** the street*
- place (direction) – ***to** the school; **up** the hill*
- means – ***by** train.*

1 Choose the preposition that you think best completes the gaps in these sentence:

    a) Are you going .... the music festival? (in / to / from).

    b) Make sure you keep your little brother .... your side at all times. (by / behind / with).

    c) We can get to the festival .... bus and then go .... the entrance to collect our tickets. (on / by / at / with / in / to).

    d) It was so exciting! I cried tears of joy when Rihanna came .... the stage. (in / by / over / on).

    e) I ran .... the front to get a better view. (on / after / to).

    f) .... the concert, we had bought some biscuits and crisps. We ate them all .... the show. Afterwards, we were still hungry so we bought a pizza .... our way home. (at / by / on / during / before / up).

2 **a)** Underline the prepositions in the paragraph below.

    b) Decide which type of preposition each one is and write them under the headings below.

> It all happened during the party. Someone had put too much chilli into the pasta, and we were soon coughing and spluttering. I knocked my fizzy drink off the table and someone slipped on the sticky mess. At school the next day, in the lunch break, we found out who was responsible - Ana. She'd had to leave the party early, before 9 o'clock, because she was going home by bus, so she hadn't seen the chaos she'd caused.

Time	Place	Means
....	....	....
....	....	....
....	....	....

4 Avoiding ambiguity

Using prepositions

Your teacher has said that your class can have an end-of-term party. Your friend, Neve, has been given the job of organising the room. But on the day of the party she is ill, so she sends you the email below:

Hi,

The tables need to go <u>over</u> the windows <u>at</u> the left-hand wall. Place the paper plates <u>next to</u> the table in piles so people can pick them up as they come in. Knives and forks need to be put <u>beyond</u> the plates. When people arrive, give them a plastic glass as they come <u>over</u> the door.

Decorations need to be hung <u>across</u> each corner of the room so they meet <u>in</u> the top of the classroom. After people are eating, make sure that there are no spilled drinks <u>under</u> the floor.

---

1. Make sense of this email by replacing the incorrect prepositions with the correct ones listed below:

   on   in   next to   on   between   under   at   through

2. Neve wants to know how the party went. Unfortunately, it was a bit of a disaster. Complete this email back to her explaining what happened:

To: Neve

Hi Neve,

Just writing to tell you all about the party. Unfortunately, it didn't go too well...........................

....

....

....

....

Use as many of these prepositions as you can. You can also make use of the word bank below.

over   under   through   next to   after   above   near   apart from   by

Word bank: *spilled, smashed, fizzy, crisps, kiwi fruit, cheese sticks, pizza slices, window, mop, cloth, unwell, fire alarm, loud, police, music*

Idioms

Idioms are common phrases used by native English speakers, often in the form of similes or metaphors. For example, 'it's bucketing down' describes heavy rain and does not mean that 'buckets' are being tipped out in the sky above!

(1) Can you match these well-known idioms to their meanings?

Idiom	Meaning
a) To add fuel to the fire	**A:** A situation in which neither side or person has an advantage.
b) His bark is worse than his bite.	**B:** Intentionally raise a false alarm.
c) To bite off more than you can chew.	**C:** Make a situation worse through what you say or do.
d) To cry wolf.	**D:** Someone who says unpleasant things but is actually not that nasty.
e) To go down like a lead balloon.	**E:** Take on more than you can cope with.
f) A level playing field.	**F:** When different people all agree on the same thing.
g) On the same page.	**G:** When a comment, joke or performance is received badly by an audience.

(2) Idioms come from lots of sources, for example, from historical activities, the works of Shakespeare, sports and so on.

Here are some sailing idioms, from a time when ships were the main means of transport. Tick what you think is the right meaning from the three choices. Look up any words you do not.

a) He runs a tight ship.

  A: Everyone with him is drunk. ☐

  B: His work or business is firmly controlled. ☐

  C: He has a belt that doesn't fit him. ☐

b) To take the wind out of someone's sails.

  A: To slow someone down or stop them, for example through pointing out their mistakes. ☐

  B: To punch someone hard. ☐

  C: To leave someone behind. ☐

c) To know the ropes.

  A: Be experienced and skilful in your job or task. ☐

  B: To know how to tie knots. ☐

  C: To enjoy sailing. ☐

d) To take a new tack.

  A: To interfere in someone's business. ☐

  B: To change direction in order to solve a problem. ☐

  C: To buy some new clothes. ☐

> **TG CD-Rom**
> Worksheet 5

3 Now, read this dialogue between two business people. What on earth are they talking about?

Jo: OK, Steve. For this meeting, we need to be singing from the same hymn sheet.

Meaning: OK, Steve. For this meeting, it is important that you and I ....

....

Steve: I agree. If we play our cards right, it'll be a piece of cake.

Meaning: If we ....

Jo: Yeah – dead easy.

Meaning: I agree, it will be ....

> **Top tip**
>
> The best use of idioms is to include them occasionally in your writing. If you use them too much, they begin to sound unnatural.

4 Write the opening two to three paragraphs of an article about the best way to deal with feeling low or sad. You could consider:
- outdoor activities
- talking to friends or family
- meditation or other relaxation methods.

Try to use three or four of these idioms in your writing, or others you can think of.
- *Run out of steam* – to be completely out of energy
- *The last straw* – when a small, final problem or burden makes everything unbearable
- *Under the weather* – to feel sick or ill
- *To be on cloud nine* – very happy
- *Wear my heart on my sleeve* – to show my emotions openly to everyone
- *Every cloud has a silver lining* – even bad things or situations can turn out well
- *Recharge your batteries* – a chance to relax and regain your energy
- *Fresh as a daisy* – to feel young and energetic

Start with:

When I'm feeling under the weather or ....

....

....

....

....

....

....

....

....

....

Comparatives

The two most common ways of comparing things are as follows:

*Let's watch the football match at home. It's **cheaper**.*

*Don't go to the stadium. It's **more expensive**.*

We tend to use *-er* for short forms, for example: *fast – faster, big – bigger.*

We also use *-er* for two-syllable words that end in *y* (when the *y* changes to *i*), for example: *tasty – tastier, funny – funnier.*

We tend to use *more* for longer **adjectives**, for example: *more spacious, more interesting, more humorous.*

We also use *more* with **adverbs** that end in *ly*, for example: *more quickly, more carefully, more thoughtfully.*

You can use *than* after comparatives, for example: *It's cheaper **than** going to the stadium.*
Or: *Going to the stadium is more expensive **than** watching it at home.*

> **Top tip**
>
> Remember that there are exceptions when forming comparatives that need to be learnt: *good/well/better; bad/badly/worse* etc.

1 Complete these sentences using a comparative form (e.g. *older, more spacious*)

a) That film last night was so boring. Can't we see something .... tonight?

b) That pizza was incredibly cheap. I expected it to be ....

c) This homework is very difficult. I expected it to be ....

d) You hardly ever walk with me to school. Why don't you walk with me .... ?

e) It's a shame my best friend has moved so far away. I wish he lived ....

2 In this letter, Rafa is writing to a friend about last year's school tennis tournament. Add the comparatives from the box below to complete the letter.

Dear Roger,

Remember how awful last year's tournament was? I hope this year's is ....
.... last year's. That weather! All that rain! It was quite light to start, but then it got .... and .... I needed an umbrella!
I won my first match easily, but the second was a real struggle. Andy hit the ball .... me. That's why I almost lost. I need to play .... Then, my game would be ....

Anyway, let's hope the sun shines and it is .... this year.
I hate playing in the cold.

See you there!
Rafa.

heavier	*warmer*	*heavier*	*harder than*	*stronger*	*better than*	*better*

4 Avoiding ambiguity

Using comparatives and superlatives

You can use *a lot, much, far* (meaning 'more'), *a bit, a little, slightly* before comparatives.
For example:

How was work today? Much better, thanks!

This homework is slightly easier than yesterday's.

This homework is far easier than yesterday's.

You can also use *any* and *no* + a comparative:

● *The door is stuck. I can't push it any harder.* (Meaning: *That is the hardest I can push it.*)
● *I expected their garden to be very big. But it's no bigger than ours.*

1 Use versions of the words in brackets to complete the following sentences:

a) I enjoyed our trip to the art gallery. It was .... I expected. (far/interesting)

b) This car is too small. I need something .... (much/big)

c) I thought she was slower than me, but in fact she's .... (slightly/quick)

Use *any* or *no* + a comparative to complete these sentences.

d) Raj had waited long enough. He wasn't going to wait ....

e) The weather isn't particularly bad today. It's .... than normal.

f) I'm sorry the music is so quiet. I can't make it ....

When using superlatives, we follow similar rules as for comparatives. We add *-est* for short words (usually adjectives) or *most* for longer words. For example:

high – highest   quick – quickest   great – greatest
difficult – most difficult   comfortable – most comfortable

Going further

2 Here is some data about three tall buildings.

	Eiffel Tower, Paris	The Shard, London	Burj Khalifa, Dubai
Height	320 metres	310 metres	828 metres
Age	Opened 1889	Opened June 2012	Opened January 2010

Write a short magazine report about famous tall buildings of the world. You could write about the age and height, comparing them.

Three world-famous buildings are the Eiffel Tower in Paris, the Burj Khalifa in Dubai

and the recently-opened Shard in London. The Shard is tall, at ....

metres, but the Eiffel Tower is .... at .... metres.

However, it isn't as .... In terms of age, the ....

of the three is ....

Prefixes

An easy and quick way to find the opposite of an **adjective** is to add a negative **prefix**. The most common are: *un, in, im, non, dis* and *mis*.

So, a *caring person* becomes an ***un**caring person* if they treat someone else badly.

These general rules may help you decide which to use, but there are exceptions:

im before a word beginning with *m* or *p* – ***immature***

ir before a word beginning with *r* – ***irrational***

il before a word beginning with *l* – ***illiterate***

Glossary

prefix – a short word or set of letters joined to the front of another word to change or add to its meaning

1 Can you add the correct prefix to the words below?

a) *in*convenient

b) ....loyal

c) ....kind

d) ....patient

e) ....possible

f) ....real

g) ....fit

h) ....logical

i) ....secure

j) ....polite

k) ....fair

l) ....organised

Some of these prefixes, especially *dis* and *mis*, can also be used with some **verbs**. So:

*My mother **approved** of my choice of car; my father **disapproved** – he thought it was too expensive.*

2 Add the correct prefix (*dis, mis* or *un* to these verbs):

a) My little brother is very naughty. He .... obeys my mother all the time.

b) I was supposed to arrive at the airport at five, but I .... timed my journey and was late!

c) Our television isn't working. When I switch it on, the picture .... appears after a few seconds.

d) By the time I left work, I only had five minutes to get to the party, so I had to .... dress in the car on the way, and put my party outfit on.

e) I loved the film, but my friend .... liked it because it was too violent.

3 There are many other prefixes which alter or add to the meaning of words. For example: *co-* (with/together) as in *co-operate*; *re-* (again), *ex* (former/before) and *inter* (between).

Add the correct prefix to the sentences below. You should be able to work out which one is needed from the context:

a) The teacher told the student to .... write his report.

b) He is divorced but he is still good friends with his ....-wife.

c) The Olympic Games represents .... national sport at its finest!

d) That bridge is so huge it has to be .... painted every year.

e) Both Tim and Jose were interested so in the end they decided to .... produce the film.

TG CD-Rom

Worksheet 6

4

Avoiding ambiguity

Useful prefixes

Knowing the meaning of some common prefixes is also very helpful when reading texts, especially those with numerical or factual information. Some typical ones include:

uni and *mono* (one)   *bi* (two)   *tri* (three)   *semi* (half)   *multi* (many)

1 Can you work out the meaning of the underlined words from the context of the sentences?

A: There was underlined_universal agreement for the plan. Unicycles would be bought for all the students!

.... and ....

B: His voice was very boring and monotonous.   ....

C: His father is Spanish, his mother Portuguese, so he's bilingual.   ....

D: Slice an orange and cut the slices into semicircles to decorate the cake.   ....

E: The company used to be based in South Korea and sell to local people, but now it's a huge multinational organisation.   ....

F: Soldiers and nurses wear uniforms; teachers don't.   ....

G: She was only semiconscious immediately after the fall, but by the time the nurse arrived she was fine.   ....

Going further

Prefixes are used to build or even create new word meanings: for example, *preview* = *pre* (before) and *view* (watch) meaning to watch something before everyone else does, usually to give an opinion – like a television critic.

2 The text below contains some words that are not made up of common prefixes but of two other words that have been brought together to create a completely new meaning.

a) Can you underline these words? The first has been done for you.

b) There are also at least three uses of common prefixes. Circle them.

> *The new heliport has been built on top of the block of flats. Unfortunately, there is so much smog that the pilots can't always land there. In fact, business people are probably better off staying at the motel on the edge of town. Of course, one alternative is to get the Chunnel under the sea between England and France, and then take the train. A rough guesstimate is that 40% of all visitors would rather take the subterranean route than fly. Of course, if you're a business person intending to drive to the UK, be very careful. Drinking and driving is strictly monitored and you may be stopped by police who carry breathalysers to check that drivers haven't been drinking. If you have been, you could be disqualified from driving.*

5 Clear punctuation

Sentence punctuation

All sentences must end with punctuation. Normally, this is a full stop.

I crashed my bicycle into the wall.

Of course, you can use other punctuation to change the meaning or tone. For example:

I crashed my bicycle into the wall! suggests surprise, shock or drama.

I crashed my bicycle into the wall? might be asked as question as the rider finds out what happened to him/her after an accident.

BUT, you cannot, of course, end with a comma. You can add further information, but you will still need a full stop when the sentence ends. For example:

I crashed into the wall, ruining my new bike forever.

(1) This student has written an exam piece about the dangers of cycling in a big city. Unfortunately, he/she has forgotten all the punctuation. Copy and rewrite this text below, putting in the correct full stops, question marks and exclamation marks where needed. You will also need to change some letters to capitals where they are at the start of a sentence.

> It is very dangerous riding a bike in our town in fact it's an absolute nightmare you would think drivers would look out for young people on bikes but they don't are we invisible or something it doesn't take half a minute for drivers to glance in their mirrors but they just don't care I wear bright clothing and make hand signals but it doesn't make any difference drivers, especially of lorries, seem to think they own the roads what are the local council going to do about it nothing as usual

Commas and apostrophes

Remember, **commas** can:

a) Separate items in a list:

I bought fajitas, tomato sauce, onions and fried chicken to prepare for the party.

b) Add or mark off adverbs, parts of sentences or phrases (often as a way of adding detail or organising your ideas):

Although I was angry, I didn't say anything.

Jose, on the other hand, believes the biggest problem is pedestrians.

Use **apostrophes** to:

a) Indicate possession.

If the 'owner' is singular, the apostrophe goes before the 's', for example:

Japan's government

My uncle's bald head

Exception: words already ending in 's': *Dickens's novels*

If the owner is plural, then the apostrophe comes after the 's', for example:

Managers' problems with their teams

Footballers' wives

Exception: special plural words: *children's, men's, women's, people's*

b) Show omission.

The apostrophe goes where a letter(s) has been removed. For example:

There isn't (is not) much you can do.

You'll (you will) be lucky!

1 Read the following text and then rewrite it adding commas and apostrophes as appropriate. If you need to change or add any words in the process, then do so.

> Even though it was raining we all went to the beach. Luka brought bread cheese salad and iced tea. Dino however brought nothing which made us all mad. Id brought a snack and so had Shan. Dinos excuse was that hed not had time to go the shop. However it didnt matter. Tourists hats were getting blown off so we knew a storm was coming and left after ten minutes.

....

....

....

....

....

....

....

Colons, semicolons, brackets and dashes

A **colon** can introduce a list, following a general statement:

We can be proud of last year: increased sales, more customers and higher profits.

It can also introduce a new part of a sentence that explains or leads on from the first part:

She was overjoyed: the bag was exactly what she wanted.

Semicolons are useful for contrasts and comparisons, and can link two simple sentences of equal importance. For example:

Irina likes table tennis; Shan prefers hockey.

1 Read this short article from a school website. Rewrite it adding colons or semicolons as appropriate.

> The new library is wonderful more shelf-space an internet zone and comfy chairs for relaxing with a favourite book. The internet zone is already popular the computers are booked up every day. Some students come early to do homework on them others use them once lessons have ended.

....

....

....

....

Brackets and **dashes** can be used to provide additional information or to make details stand out, for example, when describing a situation or event, or adding a humorous comment:

We didn't mind hanging around at the beach in the winter (despite the cold) as it was where all our friends went. Luciano (17)

Florent told us he'd bought a secondhand car – not too expensive – to replace his battered old Ford. It was secondhand – but a Ferrari!

2 Rewrite the following paragraph using dashes (or brackets!) as appropriate for additional information or for text that needs to stand out.

> It was peaceful at night except for the occasional buzzing moth and I slept like a baby. When our guide woke me at 5.30am I felt refreshed despite the time. Outside our driver a huge man in khaki shorts waited while we climbed into the jeep.

....

....

....

Top tip

Avoid **comma splicing**: this is a common error where a sentence, which should have been split up into separate sentences, or linked with another word, is mistakenly separated by a comma.

For example: *I went to see a film, it was fantastic.* This is wrong. It could be rewritten as:

I went to see a film, which was fantastic.

I went to see a film. It was fantastic.

I went to see a film: it was fantastic.

Going further

3 Write the opening two paragraphs of an article in which you give your views about tattoos. You may find these four comments from students helpful:

> Tattoos can be very individual, and give you a sense of identity.

> I like the idea of tattoos, but only ones that are temporary and can wash off.

> Once you have a tattoo, you've got it for life.

> I got a tattoo to fit in with my mates as they all have them. We had our football team's name put on the back of our hands.

Try to use the **full range of punctuation**.

You could:
- start with a question: *Do you remember the first time you saw someone …?*
- link two ideas by using a semicolon
- make a point and use brackets or dashes to show extra information or a funny aside
- use a colon to introduce a list.

Check your work as you go along – and afterwards.

1 Form, reader and purpose

Formal and informal ways of writing

It will help you complete your writing tasks effectively if you understand the **form** (the type of text), the **purpose** (what the text is for) and the **reader/audience** (who the text is for). This will also help you decide how **formal** or **informal** the text needs to be.

1 Read the following text extract.

> Dear Sir,
>
> I am writing with regard to an incident that occurred at your establishment recently. Indeed, I wish to draw your attention to the rudeness and unhelpfulness of a member of your staff on Thursday. My friend and I had gone into your so-called accessories shop, 'Bits and Pieces', to enquire whether you sold gloves of different colours (red with white spots for one hand, green with yellow stripes for the other) and your assistant, a Miss Reid, said it was ridiculous to want gloves like those, and I should try the rubbish dump! Miss Reid? More like Miss Rude! As manager, you should make sure that all your staff are fully trained and polite and …

Glossary

formal – a polite way of writing or speaking using standard vocabulary and grammar

informal – a more chatty or flexible style which uses shorter forms (such as *I'd*) and more idioms

a) What would you say is the **purpose** of this text, based on what you have read here? Tick the correct answer.

A: to enquire where the writer can buy gloves of different colours ☐

B: to complain about the writer's treatment by a member of staff at 'Bits and Pieces' ☐

C: to explain the good and bad points about the shop ☐

D: to persuade the shop manager to sack Miss Reid ☐

b) Who is the intended reader or **audience**?

A: Miss Rude ☐   C: the manager of 'Bits and Pieces' ☐

B: Miss Reid ☐   D: the writer's friend ☐

c) What **form** of text do you think this is?

A: diary ☐   D: poem ☐

B: newspaper article ☐   E: letter ☐

C: blog ☐

Going further

2 Which of these phrases from the letter is the **most formal**, in your opinion?

I am writing with regard to an incident …   *red with white spots for one hand …*

I should try the rubbish dump!

3 Here is another formal sentence from the text.

Indeed, I wish to draw your attention to the rudeness and unhelpfulness of a member of your staff on Thursday.

Rewrite a more informal version of this sentence. Choose the most informal words you can! (This is just a fun task and not something you will ever need to do for real.) Make use of words and phrases like: *dead rude, bend your ears, tell, I'd, I'm, cos.* You could begin:

Right then, ...

1 Form, reader and purpose

Different forms and styles

1 Here are some extracts from different **forms** of texts. Can you match each extract to the correct form?

a) Letter to a friend

A: The provision of a new bus route to the school from the town centre is absolutely vital. Up to 80% of traffic near the school is people dropping children off, evidence enough of the need for change.

b) Diary recounting an emotional experience

B: It'd be so cool if you could make it, and mum and dad would love to see you again. It seems ages since we've been in touch, and we're dying to see you …

c) Report in local paper of an incident

C: Today is Bangkok – I checked into the hotel this morning, 7am. Now I'm sitting in a cafe while it pours with rain outside, though it's dead hot here. Other backpackers keep on coming in, drenched through.

d) Article arguing a point of view

D: It gives me great pleasure to stand here today. When I was asked to suggest someone to open the new gallery, it was a real honour …

e) Blog from a trip

E: Don't know where you'll be when you read this, but I can hardly find the words to tell you what happened today; I don't want to make a mountain out of a molehill, but …

f) Speech to introduce someone

F: The whole street was closed for at least five hours as fire-fighters fought vainly to save the carpet shop, belonging to the Manzoor brothers …

2 Some of the clues to the type of text come from the degree of formality and informality each uses. A report in a newspaper is more likely to be formal, for example. Look at the task again and copy below any examples of the following features you can see:

a) Contractions – *I'll, we'd, don't*

....

b) Shorter, chatty sentences or phrases – *Next stop, London …*

....

c) Slang, or 'teenage-speak' – *cool, fab*

....

d) Idiom: common images used to describe something – *every cloud has a silver lining; he was frozen out of the conversation*

....

3 Your local council wants to reduce the number of buses from villages outside coming into the town centre. Here are some views about this plan:

- *Money is tight. We need to cut non-essential services.*
- *Older people often don't drive. The bus is their link to life.*
- *People should be encouraged to walk or use bicycles.*
- *Villagers bring vital trade to the town. If they stay at home, they'll just shop on the internet.*

Write an article for your local newspaper giving your views about the issue.

Based on this information, answer the questions below:

a) What is the **form/type** of text you need to write? ....

b) What will be the **purpose** of the text? (Think carefully – there may be more than one.)

....

c) Who are the **readers** likely to be? ....

4 How **formal** do you think the text in task 1 will need to be? Circle the correct choice below. Think about the readers – are they friends, family, your community?

Very informal   Quite informal   Quite formal   Very formal

5 One student has begun their response to the task in this way:

<u>Yeah</u>, well <u>it's dead obvious, bro'</u>, that we need to look at all the different views about buses. Because people disagree, don't they? It's not as straightforward as we all think. Like, there's those – like old folks – who need them to get around. Then, there's others who should be getting off their backsides and getting exercise. Take me – I'm really lazy, and I live in a village, so it'd do me good to hop on my bike, break a sweat. Know what I'm saying? Course you do.

Underline any examples of informal words or phrases. The first two have been done for you.

6 Has the student got the type/form of text right? Which of these does the text seem to be?

A: an email ☐

B: the transcript of a conversation ☐

C: an article in a paper ☐

7 Which type of text should it be? ....

Going further

8 Write an alternative, more formal, first paragraph for the writing task. Use this prompt to get you started:

The problem of bus provision has led to many different opinions being expressed...

....

....

....

....

1 Form, reader and purpose

(9) You have just visited the new art gallery in your local town. In it, there is a very surprising work of modern art.

After the visit, you decide to write a letter to your brother/sister, who now lives overseas, describing what you saw. In your letter you should:

- say who you went with
- describe the work of art
- give your opinion of it.

The style and vocabulary you choose will need to match the form, purpose and reader.

You have been told the form – a **letter**.

Now, check you are clear about the reader and purpose(s) by filling in the spaces below:

Your reader: ....

Purpose: ....

(10) Here are some extracts from students responses to the task. Decide whether each extract is of the appropriate level of formality. Then circle the answer 'yes', 'no' or 'maybe':

a) Correct reader?

A: You know that new art-gallery that opened just after you left?   yes   no   maybe

B: There is a new art-gallery in the town where I live, and ...   yes   no   maybe

C: I am delighted to inform you about some important news about the art-gallery, which you are no doubt aware of ...   yes   no   maybe

b) Correct purpose(s)?

A: Wednesday. Visited the new cafe at the art gallery. Really great! Spent two hours there, sampling all the different cakes and candy. Didn't hang around long, as there's this tennis match I want to watch on television tonight, so ...   yes   no   maybe

B: You'll probably remember that a gallery opened a few weeks after you left. Well, I have put off going there as art is not really my cup of tea. But Leo persuaded me, and he was right. There was this incredible steel sculpture – it's basically an upside-down ...   yes   no   maybe

C: The new art-gallery is open from 10 till 6 everyday. Visitors can browse the gift-shop, wander around the free exhibition, or stop for refreshments in the rooftop cafe. There are a number of popular art-works, including, 'Boat' by Morgan Z.   yes   no   maybe

(11) Which of the extracts A, B or C is closest to the letter asked for in task 7 ....

> **TG CD–Rom**
> Worksheet 7

Going further

(12) Now, on a separate piece of paper, write your letter in response to the task. Use the opening you chose above, or your own ideas.

2 Variety of structures

You can use different sentence and paragraph structures to achieve different effects in your writing. For example, you could use a short final sentence after longer ones to repeat or emphasise the first main point.

I believe you can never have too many friends. You need friends for every occasion, for example, when you feel low, or for when you want to share good news, or when you want someone to tell you the truth. **Having lots of friends is great.**

1 Here is a similar text. Can you add a simple, short, final sentence which has a similar purpose to the ones you have read?

I really don't enjoy visiting big, busy, indoor shopping centres. I find that the lack of natural light,

the crowds, the people fighting to get a bargain all get too much for me. ....

....

2 Now read another text.

I believe you can never have too many friends. You need friends for every occasion, for example, when you feel low, or for when you want to share good news. But most important of all is a friend who will tell you the truth when you need it. **You need someone who is honest.**

What is the purpose of the short final sentence in this case? Tick the correct answer.

A: to add a new point ☐

B: to stress or emphasise the first point ☐

C: to disagree with an earlier point ☐

D: to emphasise the point in the third sentence ☐

3 Now look at a similar idea, extended into two paragraphs, the second one a single sentence.

I believe you can never have too many friends. Friends for every occasion, for example when you feel low, or for when you want to share good news. But most important of all, you need a friend who will tell you the truth when you need it. Someone who is honest.

This person may well be the most important person in your life, the person who helps you make good decisions.

What is the purpose of this single-sentence second paragraph here?
Tick the correct box.

A: to begin a completely new idea which is unconnected to the previous paragraph ☐

B: to take an idea from the first paragraph and develop it in more detail ☐

C: to cover all the points again from the first paragraph ☐

4 Short sentences can be used for different reasons. In the example, below one student describes a working holiday he took on a farm.

The old man watched me from his old wooden stool every morning as I struggled to capture the stray goats and herd them into the rickety pen nearby. He said nothing, and betrayed no emotions as I stumbled here and there, trying to round them up. Then, one morning, he stood up.

Why is the final sentence in this paragraph a short one?

A: to draw the reader's attention to a change in the old man's behaviour ☐

B: because the student has run out of things to say ☐

C: to repeat an earlier point – how the old man keeps on standing up ☐

Going further

(5) What do you think is going to happen when the old man stands up? There are some clues in the text, such as the writer being unable to herd the cattle properly.

Write your ideas here:

I think that ....

(6) Now write the next paragraph. You could make it a one-sentence one, which focuses on the old man and what he does next. Start...

The old man ....

....

....

> **Top tip**
>
> Single short sentences are all about making the reader follow your ideas. You can have an impact on what the reader thinks or feels. So, use them for dramatic effect (a sudden change or development), to emphasise an idea/event, and to develop an idea by adding detail.

Time order

If you are recounting an event – a visit, a trip, something that happened to you or someone you know – you would normally tell the events in **time order**.

> **A:** *I must tell you about my school trip **yesterday**. I arrived at the gallery at 10am and **then** started to look around. **Eventually**, I came to a room with this incredible sculpture in it – a steel eagle ...*

However, sometimes you can change the order around for effect:

> **B:** *Imagine this incredible, hanging sculpture made of steel in the shape of an eagle. Well, that is what I saw as I walked into the room at the gallery. We had gone there that morning with the school, but I wasn't expecting much when we first arrived at 10am. We looked around a bit, but I wasn't that impressed.*

(1) On the left below you will see the order of paragraph A. In the box on the right, list the order of the second account (paragraph B) as it is told.

Tells about yesterday, gallery at 10am

Starts to look around

Then, into room/sees sculpture

2 In this exam-style task, Ines was asked to write an article about 'My secret place' for her school magazine. She has decided to write about a secret lake in some nearby woods.

Here are the notes for her plan in the order she decided to write her article:

1. When and where I first found 'My secret lake'
2. What it looked like
3. Why I don't go there now
4. Where I go now for time to myself

3 Here's the opening to Ines's article:

I first found my own secret place when I was nine years' old. I was with my older brother and sister, exploring our local woods, when I got lost. I wandered around, and eventually found myself in a clearing. I could hear water …

Here's an alternative opening:

Having a secret place to go to think for yourself is very important. Nowadays, I tend just to go to my room, put my headphones on, and listen to music. But, once, I had my own special, secret place to go …

Both texts work well, but what is the difference between the two? Write your answer below.

The first opening tells us straightaway about ....

....

The second opening is different because it ....

....

Going further

4 Here is a plan that you could use for the article. Add further details of your own. (You don't have to use any of Ines's ideas above.)

a) When and where I first found it (time, my age, where, who with – if anyone)

....

....

....

b) What it looked like (e.g. description of nature/things I saw there; my feelings/why it helped me)

....

....

....

c) Why I don't go there now (when I stopped going there and why, e.g. other kids/I grew up)

....

....

....

d) Where I go now for time to myself (e.g. my room; a new 'secret place')

....

....

....

Now you have your plan, you can decide which section to begin with. You do not have to start with section a); you could start with section d) for variety. From and older viewpoint, you could look back at your younger self.

Write your article for your school magazine on a separate piece of paper.

Try to include variety in other ways too. Think about using:

- short sentences for effect/drama
- paragraphs of different lengths
- building in descriptive details (see page 49–52).

Variety when writing to argue or persuade

Your school has been offered sponsorship by a big fast-food company. It will bring lots of money to the school which desperately short of funds, but in return the fast-food company wants to install vending machines in all the corridors, and serve its food in the canteen.

Write a letter to your school principal giving your views on this issue.

There are many ways you could start your letter. But first, you need to decide your viewpoint. Choose one of these:

It's completely wrong – no way!   *I don't really agree, but...*

It could work, but...   *It's a great idea!*

You could begin by expressing your point of view **very strongly** in the first topic sentence:

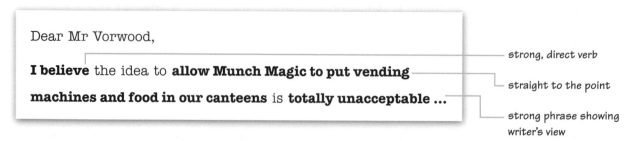

Dear Mr Vorwood,

I believe the idea to **allow Munch Magic to put vending machines and food in our canteens** is **totally unacceptable ...**

— strong, direct verb
— straight to the point
— strong phrase showing writer's view

1 Now, write a similar strong first sentence against the idea. Select the strongest verbs and phrases from those provided, and write the new sentence below:

> I (am convinced/am certain/think/wonder if) the idea to allow Munch Magic to put vending machines and food in our canteens is (utterly ridiculous/totally wrong/rather bad/a bit of a mistake).

I ....

....

2 Expressing your viewpoint so clearly at the start of your letter might not be the best way to persuade your principal. You could begin by mentioning the apparent good points:
- the school needs money
- lots of students like fast food
- new ways of finding funds are important

So, for variety and effect, you could start:

> Dear Mr Vorwood,
>
> I am fully aware that the school needs money, and that ...

Complete the paragraph:

....

....

Then, you could add:

> However, I strongly believe that ...

Complete the sentence:

....

....

TG CD-Rom

Worksheet 8

Read this article about falconry and then complete the tasks that follow.

Falconry, is the act of hunting animals in their natural habitat through the use of a trained bird of prey, often a falcon (a type of hawk), hence the name. A centuries-old activity, it is now mostly used for exhibitions and shows, in which trained falconers let the falcon loose and it returns to its trainer to a range of commands or actions. It can be incredibly dramatic to watch as the falcons swoop down from trees or high in the air to retrieve the morsel of food the falconer offers them.

Phil Wagner has been a falconer for almost 15 years. 'Most people realise that falconry is an ancient sport. But they're fascinated when they see me working with my falcon up close. It's an incredibly close connection between a falconer and his or her falcon.'

Phil explains how the training begins with '**manning**', that is, getting the hawk used to your presence. Once the hawk trusts you as a loyal provider of food, and is used to its new surroundings, it will feed calmly on your gloved fist and training can begin. The hawk now has to learn to come to you for food. First, it needs to be attached to a line – called a **creance** – and placed on a post or an assistant's hand. Then, you hold a piece of meat in your gloved fist so the hawk can see it. To start with, it will probably only come a very short distance, but after a few days you can increase the distance to about 50–100m. When the hawk comes this far without hesitation, you are ready to let it fly freely. Then, using a **lure** – a line with meat at the end – you can train it to follow or come to you as you swing the lure in the air.

The specialised words shown in bold go back many, many years – in fact, back to the 16th century. Shakespeare included a speech in his play *The Taming of the Shrew*

in which the main character talks about how he is going to tame his wife as if she were a hawk. Not very nice at all!

This just shows that falconry is an ancient sport and remains very popular in many cultures around the world. Many different species of hawk are used, from the Northern Goshawk and Peregrine Falcon, to the widely used Harris Hawk and the Red-Tailed Hawk. In the Middle East, the Saker Falcon is the traditional choice, although Peregrines are widely used, too. The UAE is said to spend over 27 million dollars each year towards the conservation of wild falcons. For example, there are two breeding farms in the Emirates, as well as in Qatar and Saudi Arabia.

Medieval falconers often rode horses, but this is now rare, with the exception of a few Eastern European countries. In Kazakhstan, Kyrgyzstan and Mongolia, for example, the Golden Eagle is traditionally flown from horseback, hunting creatures as large as foxes and wolves.

Phil says that people tend to think of falconry as simply an ancient craft which is now only done for entertainment. 'Far from it. My main source of income is not doing shows for people, but actually working with local schools. Many of them are plagued by seagulls, which create mess and nest on school buildings. Every week I visit the schools and 'Leon', my hawk, drives them away. We don't actually catch the gulls, but our presence is enough to drive them off to find other nesting places.'

1. Your school has asked for suggestions for activities at a school open day. You wish to suggest having a falconry display but you need to explain to the School Council what it is.

Make two short notes under each of the headings below.

What falconry is

....

....

How falconers train their hawks

....

....

What hawks are used for apart from for demonstrations

....

....

3 Writing to summarise

2) Imagine you have given your talk to the School Council. Next, you wish to produce a written summary to remind them of the details of the talk.

Using your notes from task 1, write a summary about the art of falconry, and how falconers train their hawks. You should write no more than 70 words.

Going further

You have been asked to provide a longer written summary about falconry.

3 You will need to read through the article on pages 74–75 again. Use the following headings to help you plan your written summary.

Falconry in the past

....

....

....

How falcons are trained

....

....

....

Falconry today

....

....

....

4 Now write your summary in 100–120 words. **E**

....

....

....

....

....

....

....

....

....

....

....

....

....

Writing to inform and explain

When you write to explain something, the most important things are:

- logical structure – using the right verb tenses (e.g. future, present) and choosing appropriate sentence lengths
- clear expression – ensuring your explanation makes sense by choosing the right words and appropriate vocabulary.

Read this text:

> *Many children feel afraid of the dark. A child's fear may disrupt their bedtime routine and sleep. There are many ways that parents can help their child to overcome this common fear. A nightlight, comforters such as a toy or teddy and a bedtime routine can help. Take a child's fears seriously but do not pretend to check for monsters as this may suggest to the child you believe monsters could exist.*

From http://www.betterhealth.vic.gov.au

1 Write down the **short topic sentence** that introduces the main idea of this paragraph:

....

2 Write down **three** further examples of **present tense verbs** that show this is an informative piece of writing:

There are many ways ....

....

3 Write down **four** items of **vocabulary** specifically-related to children's bedtime used in the passage: the first has been selected for you:

Nightlight ....

....

4 Imagine you have been asked to write a letter to a friend who is going on a safari in the African bush. He or she has trouble sleeping, and is worried about the wild animals outside the tent.

Select, from this bank of words, vocabulary that would be suitable for this letter. Then put the words beneath the relevant heading below.

> **Word bank:** *creatures, camping lamp, torch, book, sleeping bag, mosquito net, insects, creepy-crawlies, shadows, camp leader, jeep, campfire, undergrowth, dreams, friends, lions, sounds*

Fears	Equipment	People	Sleep	The campsite

These headings could form the basis for the paragraphs you write. For example:

Paragraph 1:   fears

Paragraph 2:   people who can help you

Paragraph 3, 4, 5

5 Now put the paragraphs in a logical order. Would you deal with or mention fears first? Or refer to the campsite? There is no 'right' answer, but you must decide.

6 Next, select the present tense verbs in these sentences that you might write in the letter, then write the correct version of the verb underneath:

a) It <u>is/was</u> a good idea to make sure you <u>zip/zipped</u> the tent up properly.

....

b) If you <u>hear/heard</u> sounds outside, <u>didn't/don't</u> <u>worry/worried</u>, as most creatures <u>keep/kept</u> away from campsites because of the fire.

....

c) You <u>can/were able to</u> help yourself sleep by <u>listening/listened</u> to relaxing music on your MP3 player. Or you <u>can/could</u> just <u>chat/chatted</u> about pop music or television programmes with your friends to <u>took/take</u> your mind off things.

....

....

d) If you really <u>can't/were unable to</u> get to sleep, then <u>go/went</u> and <u>sat/sit</u> by the campfire with the camp leader.

....

....

7 Now write the whole letter, apart from the last paragraph, using the sentences above or new ones of your own. Write the paragraphs in the order you decided on in task 5.

Dear Istvan,

....

....

....

....

....

Going further

Write the final paragraph of the letter to your friend. You could say something about using his torch, or reassure him again about the noises he hears.

Finally, Istvan, you can ....

....

....

4 Writing to inform and explain

Your parents have asked you to help clear out a room in an older relative's flat. You are not that keen to do it as you do not know your relative very well and whenever you see him/her they seem really boring. However, when you clear out the room, you find many interesting things and learn a lot about your relative and their life.

Write an article for your local newspaper on the theme of 'not judging someone by first appearances'. Base it on what you found in your relative's room.

8 First, plan what you could write about under these headings:

Memories of your relative

....

....

The room on first appearance

....

....

Three objects you found that revealed something about your relative

A: ....

....

B: ....

....

C: ....

....

Your feelings about your relative after you cleared out the room

....

....

....

9 Now, write your article in 200 words in the space below. You could use:

- **connectives** or other phrases to contrast or compare a change in the way you think about something, for example:

  I used to think that my uncle was cruel. **However/But/Now** *...*

  If *you believe that all old people are boring, then you will be surprised by ...*

  Despite *how I felt, I was shocked when ...*

- **clear verbs in the present tense** that show your clear thinking now, for example:

  We **must consider** *...*

  I **believe that** *...*

5 Writing to argue a point of view

When you write to present a particular point of view, you need lots of points to make, both for and against the idea.

Imagine you are going to write an article for your school or college magazine giving your views on whether we should preserve endangered species. You have interviewed some experts about the issue and here are some of their comments:

- *Charity leader: 'I think more money is needed to support species under threat.'*
- *Presenter of TV programme on animals: 'People are too obsessed with certain "cuddly" rare animals.'*
- *Warden of National Park: 'If we just allow a species to die out, why will anyone bother to protect the rest?'*
- *Teacher: 'Rare species are important but we must spend money on humans first.'*

Your article should be 150–200 words long.

Generating ideas

1 First, complete this concept map, which includes some of the arguments from the comments above.

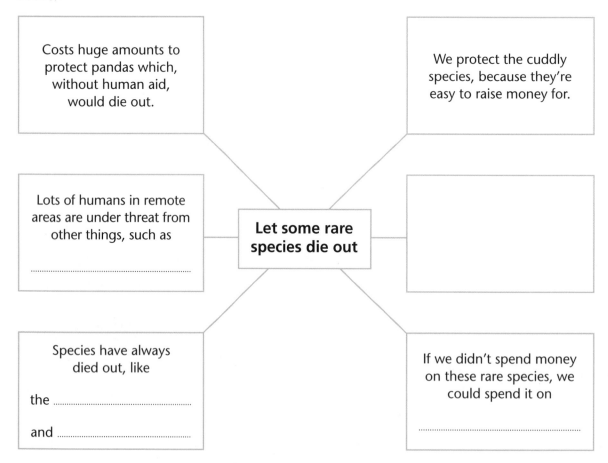

Costs huge amounts to protect pandas which, without human aid, would die out.

We protect the cuddly species, because they're easy to raise money for.

Lots of humans in remote areas are under threat from other things, such as

....

Let some rare species die out

Species have always died out, like

the ....

and ....

If we didn't spend money on these rare species, we could spend it on

....

2 Now, complete the concept map on page 83 with points *for* spending money on preserving endangered species. You can include the ones from the comments and add your own.

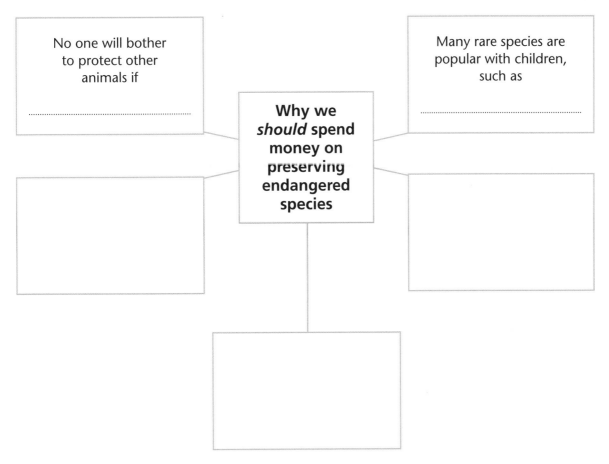

No one will bother to protect other animals if

....

Why we *should* spend money on preserving endangered species

Many rare species are popular with children, such as

....

3 Now you have your points and evidence, you need to build paragraphs. The first paragraph of your article should be quite general. Read these three versions by different students and then write the correct letters in the boxes in a) and b) below.

Mark

It is clear to me that it is wrong to spend money on animals that have little chance of survival naturally. These animals, like pandas, are not suited to modern environments and it is wrong to keep them alive for our pleasure and entertainment.

Ayeesha

This is, like, totally wrong. The idea that people think we should spend less on rare species is bonkers!!! I am completely against it. I love fluffy-wuffy animals …

Ryad

The subject of spending on endangered species is a very difficult one, as there are many arguments on both sides. Whether you are an animal lover or not, everyone should have a view on whether we should spend money on preserving particular species, or let them die out naturally.

a) Which one:

   A: introduces the argument clearly and reasonably?

   B: sounds balanced and clear on the issues/is not for one side or the other?

   C: is not balanced – just expresses one side of the argument?

   Ayeesha's ☐   Ryad's ☐   Mark's ☐

b) Which one(s):

   A: uses appropriate language?

   B: uses language that is too informal?

   Ayeesha's ☐   Ryad's ☐   Mark's ☐

Writing to argue a point of view

Linking points using connectives

1 Look at these examples and evidence. Decide which example or evidence leads to the idea or viewpoint on the other side. Draw lines between them.

Example/evidence

a) *Rare species, like the Yangtze river dolphin, died out and no one made a fuss because it wasn't pretty.*

b) *Some animals require lots of land and human help. Without us, they would die out.*

c) *Focusing on pandas, tigers and whales means other areas of nature are ignored.*

Viewpoint

A: *We should spend money on species that stand a chance of survival.*

B: *Campaigns should focus more on insects, plants and trees.*

C: *We shouldn't only preserve cuddly-looking animals.*

2 Now write the linked sentences below using connectives such as:

therefore   so   because   as a result

a) *Rare species like the Yangtze river dolphin died out and no one made a fuss because it wasn't*

  pretty, therefore ....

b) *Some animals require lots of land and human help. Without us, they would die out, so* ....

  ....

c) *Focusing on pandas, tigers and whales means other areas of nature are ignored* ....

  ....

Next make your own further point using other connectives, such as, *as a result, this means that, so*

d) ....

  ....

3 Now write **three** sentences in favour of spending money on endangered species. Again, use connectives where they are needed.

a) It is important that we preserve animals such as the giant panda ....

  ....

b) If we don't spend money on well-known endangered species, ...

  ....

c) Another thing we need to be aware of is ....

  ....

Top tip

Many of these argument-style sentences are about cause and effect. *If we do this, then that ...*
This is a really useful phrase to use in this kind of essay.

The end of your article

You could end your article by giving your final point of view to your readers. You could choose one of these paragraph starters then give your viewpoint. Write your final paragraph below.

Finally, I believe that …

In general, I think it is true that …

My final point is that we should …

At the end of the day, I feel strongly that …

....

....

....

....

....

....

....

....

Going further

A good argument piece is not just be about giving your points and evidence. It must also have an emotional impact, especially if you are trying to persuade your reader. You can do this by adding:
- personal experience or anecdote (this can be made up – it needn't have actually happened to you)
- visual imagery.

1 **a)** What is the difference between these two students' responses to the task?

Lia

I remember my first visit to a zoo to see a panda. Those huge dark eyes staring out at me, pleading with me. The panda was on his own, as there was no mate for him. I felt so sorry for him.

Luis

Pandas are often brought up in zoos on their own until they die because there is no mate for them. It is very sad.

b) Underline the personal anecdote in Lia's version and her use of visual details.

2 Now, write your own 'made-up' personal anecdote based on seeing an endangered animal either in the wild or in a zoo. You can choose one of these starters or write your own:
- *It was when I was about five that I first saw …*
- *One day, when I was …*
- *I have a memory that sticks in my mind. My family and I were …*

6 Writing a personal description of an experience

Read how one student describes a terrible journey to a holiday destination in a letter home to a friend.

Dear Juan,

We've arrived at last, but I must tell you about our terrible journey![1] As you know, I've been looking forward to this holiday for weeks. Do you remember how I crossed off each date on the calendar as the holiday got nearer?[2] Well, yesterday when we caught the bus to the airport I finally relaxed. One quick bus ride, and we'd be on the plane. How wrong could I be?[3]

The bus ride to the airport was dreadful![4] We had roadworks, a demonstration by some students, and even a herd of fat cattle who wouldn't move! I thought we weren't going to make it. Dad spent most of the time beeping his horn and shaking his fist at anyone and everyone. In contrast,[5] Mum sat there very calmly. They're like chalk and cheese![6] Her view is, 'what will be, will be'.

Finally,[7] you'll be pleased to hear, we made it to check-in. As we queued up I could see the look of relief on Dad's face. At the desk,[8] the assistant looked at us blankly when we handed over our passports and ticket printout. 'Your flight is tomorrow, not today,' she said, pointing to the date on our tickets.

So, the truth is I'm writing this from the airport.[9] We have arrived – just not in the right place! But hopefully, by the time you actually read these words, we'll really be there, sitting by the hotel pool! But for now my bed is a hard, cold plastic chair.[10]

I'll send a postcard, or email you when I have some proper holiday news!

Bye for now,

Pavla

1 These are the excellent skills that the student has used. Write the correct number from the text above in the boxes by the descriptions below.

a) Short question links to next paragraph ☐

b) Topic sentence introduces the idea of the journey and how the writer felt about it ☐

c) Clear vivid description helps us see the situation ☐

d) Connective helps us compare Dad and Mum ☐

e) Good use of direct question and 'you' to show this is a letter to a friend ☐

f) Sequence word introduces next stage of the personal account ☐

g) Preposition helps us picture where this takes place ☐

h) Good idiom which shows how different the parents are ☐

i) New topic sentence introduces terrible bus ride ☐

j) Final paragraph brings us up to date ☐

Note how the **cohesion** in this text is created by each of the four paragraphs: they are about different things, but all linked to the same subject – the awful journey.

2 Here is a list of possible paragraph titles for the letter on page 86. Four of them are correct.

Select the four titles you think match each paragraph's content in the letter and circle 'suitable'.

A: The nice calendar in our kitchen	suitable	not suitable
B: How I was looking forward to our holiday	suitable	not suitable
C: Mum and Dad's wedding	suitable	not suitable
D: An uncomfortable bed for the night	suitable	not suitable
E: The food we ate on the way	suitable	not suitable
F: A mistake at check-in	suitable	not suitable
G: Forgetting our passports	suitable	not suitable
H: An awful car ride with mum and dad	suitable	not suitable
I: Why I love airports	suitable	not suitable

3 Now, write the correct order for the four paragraphs here:

Paragraph 1 ....

Paragraph 2 ....

Paragraph 3 ....

Paragraph 4 ....

Top tip

In personal descriptions, especially ones in which several things happen, the texts are usually linked by time phrases, for example *finally*.

Real fluency in writing comes when you do not need to repeat words or ideas that you are certain the reader understands or remembers: for example, 'airport' is mentioned in paragraphs 1 and 2 so it does not need to be repeated when 'check-in' is mentioned in paragraph 3.

6 Writing a personal description of an experience

4 Write part of a new letter from Pavla. She has arrived safely at the hotel, but she has a terrible trip to the beach. Describe what happened. Write the second and third paragraphs of that letter, following on from the opening below.

Try to use some of the skills you looked at in detail from Pavla's original letter on page 86.

Dear Juan,

This holiday gets worse! We got to our hotel without a problem, had a good night's sleep and then woke up to lovely sunshine and a nice cool breeze. I know this sounds fine, but wait a moment! Time for a trip to the beach, we all thought, so we took our towels, suncream, some snacks and drinks, and set off.

The problem was ....

....

....

....

....

....

....

....

....

....

....

....

....

Here are some ideas you could use for your second and third paragraphs, or use your own:
- getting lost
- forgetting something or someone
- changes in the weather
- a silly accident.

Remember: the following connectives will help link your ideas both within and between paragraphs. The main uses are:
- time order sequence – *at first, next, later that day*
- simple ordering of events or actions – *firstly, secondly, finally*
- logical ordering (often related to cause and effect) – *therefore, as a result, because of this*
- contrast – *on the other hand, in contrast, however, although*
- development of ideas – *what is more, in addition, moreover.*

Going further

You have seen how a really good personal description contains:

- clear, fluent expression; the reader can follow the ideas and events in and between paragraphs
- ideas and events that are linked so they all fit the 'theme' or situation
- clear description – images or things described as if in 'close-up'
- prepositions that help the reader see how things or events are related or connected
- clear paragraphs that each contain different ideas or information, but which are linked by the overall story or description
- a tone or style that fits the form of the text (for example, letter, article).

(5) Imagine that your younger brother or sister took part in a charity fun-run to raise money for your school. During the fun-run something interesting happened.

You have been asked to write a report about it for your school magazine.

In your article you should:

- describe what you saw
- explain how you felt and reacted
- tell the readers what happened in the end.

The photographs may give you some ideas, but you are free to use any ideas of your own.

Your article should be between 150 and 200 words long. You can include a title for your report if you wish.

You will receive equal marks for the content of your letter and for the style and accuracy of your language.

Now write your article below:

....

....

....

....

....

....

....

....

....

....

....

....

1 Key question words

Questioning words

Very often, listening questions will include key question words which will help you work out the information you need to give.

> **Where** questions usually mean giving the name of a place, (such as *the station, Jon's house*).
>
> **Who** questions mean you need to give a person's name or role/job in your answer (for example, *Who has a key for the mystery door? The shopkeeper.*).
>
> **When** questions are usually about a specific time (for example, *2pm, late afternoon, after the show*).
>
> **How many?** relates to a number of people, objects or times (*How many are going to the show? How many times will Suresh need to visit the hospital?*).
>
> **What?** can be linked to time, number or a range of things, so listen carefully for more information.
>
> **Why?** involves looking for reasons, causes, explanations (for example, *Why did Anya get up early?*).

① Can you add the correct question word into these typical questions? (At least one of these could have more than one question word.)

a) .... does the bus stop before it reaches Jo's street?

b) .... will the plane take off, morning or afternoon?

c) .... did Raj change his mind about going to the party?

d) .... reason did Soraya give for being late?

e) .... will meet Ben at the end of his round-the-world trip?

f) .... times has Lucy been swimming this week?

② Below is the transcript of a short listening exercise. Create five questions using a different question word each time:

Manesh: Hi Vijay. Sorry I missed your call – I was out walking the dog and only just got back. Can you do me a favour?

Vijay: Of course. What is it?

Manesh: There's no way I can get to the station to pick up Mum at 5pm. Could you get her for me? She said she'll wait by the hot-dog stand.

Vijay: I'll take your car. Is that ok?

Manesh: No – she's got three large cases so you'll need to take the family car. Thanks!

Write your questions here:

1: <u>Where was Manesh</u> ....

2: ....

3: ....

4: ....

5: ....

Spotting the clues in the questions

There are usually one or more key words in the questions, as well as the 'what', 'where', 'why' ones, which help you decide what you will have to listen out for in the recording.

For example, if the question is: *What is the earliest time you can catch a bus?* You know your answer will definitely be a time. What you want is a specific *time* – so you could underline *earliest time* as a key phrase.

But there are other words too: *you can catch a bus*. It's clear you will need to listen for information about 'buses' and when they leave/depart. You may want to underline *bus* in the question too.

1 Underline the key words in these three questions:

a) How many seats are available for the concert?

b) What is the highest peak Shona has climbed?

c) When will the cafe be ready to re-open?

2 Imagine that you have heard the speaker say:

The buses give a good service. They run all day until midnight, after the cinemas close. On the other hand, you can catch the earliest one to get to town before the shops open. That bus leaves at 7am.

Now answer the question:

What is the earliest time you can catch a bus? ....

Sometimes you may hear similar information that you do not need, so take care. Here's some more from the same transcript.

The buses give a good service. They run all day until midnight, after the cinemas close. On the other hand, you can catch the earliest one to get to town before the shops open. That bus leaves at 7am, but the trains are better; the earliest train leaves at 6.30am.

3 A student called Jamie gave the answer: *6.30am.* Why do you think Jamie got this wrong?

I think he got it wrong because he noticed ....

....

4 Now listen to this final text. (4.1)

Highlight the key words in these questions and then answer them:

a) What is the earliest time you can get a tram? ....

b) Which form of transport takes the longest to get to town? ....

c) What time of day or night do the buses stop running? ....

2 Predicting answers, using inference

When you hear short snippets of speech on a recording, it will help you if you can work out where the people are meant to be. For example, if you know they are supposed to be in a coffee shop, be prepared to think of all the vocabulary likely to be linked to coffee shops, rather than airports, schools or hospitals.

1 Practise focusing on vocabulary groups by completing this table with possibilities for what you might hear. The first row has been done for you.

You hear a person say	At least one person is probably in	Some words/phrases that you may hear or need to use
Shall we have a pizza?	A restaurant or a food takeaway shop	toppings; cheese; cost; delivery service; mushrooms; tomato
	A dentist's surgery	
Where is your homework?		
		platform; announcement; delay; on time; waiting room; ticket office
	A cinema	
	A college or university	

2 When you have finished, add:

   a) another example of your own to the list in the bottom row

   b) three extra words to each set of words in column 3.

3 You have practised highlighting key words. Now have another go with these questions. What are the key words in these questions that would help you identify the right details?

   a) What is the colour of the dress Maria is going to buy?

   b) How much does it cost to buy a return airline ticket to Moscow?

   c) In which year was the World Championship held in Istanbul?

   d) How much did the horse which stood on Erik's foot weigh?

   e) How far did the young man have to walk through the snow when his car broke down?

   f) What is the sculpture made out of?

4 Now have a 'mad guess' at the answers. You won't *know* of course, because you haven't heard the conversations. But by doing your pre-listening work, you will still be able to have a go and you will see if the *type* of answer you give is correct.

My 'mad guesses'

a) .Purple with white spots!...

b) ....

c) ....

d) ....

e) ....

f) ....

5 Did you have any answers ending with: pounds, dollars, euros, kg, tons, km, miles, yards or metres? Which questions (a to f) could these words be a part of the answer to?

Write the letters here: ...., ... and ....

6 Imagine my mad guesses were those given below. Write next to each one the letter of the question it could be the answer to. One of them has been done for you.

1954   ....

purple with white spots   ...a)...........

stone   ....

200km   ....

2 tons   ....

500 dollars   ....

7 Now you can test yourself.

Listen to the dialogues once and answer what you can. Then give yourself 30 seconds to check your answers and focus your mind on what parts you will have to listen to extra carefully on the second listening. Then play the recording a second time. This is your chance to double-check your answers and to fill in any gaps.

4.2

a) What is the colour of the dress Maria is going to buy? ....

b) How much does it cost to buy a return airline ticket to Moscow? ....

c) In which year was the World Championship held in Istanbul? ....

d) How much did the horse which stood on Erik's foot weigh? ....

e) How far did the speaker have to walk after his car broke down? ....

f) What is the sculpture made out of? ....

Units of measurement

Listening tasks will always include some questions where you are asked for numbers and some kind of measurement, such as:

height/length/distance: *feet and inches; millimetres, centimetres metres and kilometres*

weight: *pounds, ounces and tons; milligrams, grams, kilograms and tonnes*

cost: *pounds, dollars, euros, dinars, rupees etc.*

times: *am or pm; hours, minutes and seconds*

Top tip

Ensure that you know all these words for measurements and can spell them correctly. Use a dictionary for any you are unsure of. Always include the unit of measurement, for example: *grams, dollars*. If you just give a number, it does not answer the question properly and you will not get any marks!

1 Here are some answers to the listening questions you did on page 93.

Write what mark you would give each answer and say why. Each question is worth one mark. Remember, you are looking for an answer which shows they understood what they heard.

Question number	The right answer	Answer to be marked	Your mark	Reason
b)	600 euros	six hundred euros		
		E600		
		600		
d)	700kg (*or* kilograms)	700		
		700 kilos		
e)	10km (*or* kilometres)	10		
		ten kilometres		
		10 miles		

2 Now check the answers you gave and see if you remembered to include the correct units of measurement for these questions.

3 Keeping the answers brief

For some listening questions, you must try to keep your answers short and exact. It is just the same as when you were preparing for the reading questions.

Here are some answers from students who answered the same questions as you did.

Q: *What is the colour of the dress Maria is going to buy?*

A: The red roses on the skirt here are so pretty. But the blue one is definitely.

1 Why do you think a student gave this answer? Tick the best explanation below.

a) The student didn't know the correct answer and so just wrote down anything to do with colour. ☐

b) The student knew the answer but wanted to give extra information for an extra mark. ☐

c) The student didn't understand the question at all. ☐

2 Another student wrote:

The blue one is definitely more suitable. Yes that's the one.

Is this a good answer? Tick the statement you agree with.

A: Yes, it's the right answer and could not be improved. ☐

B: Yes, it's the right answer but the student has wasted time by including unnecessary words. ☐

C: No, it's the wrong answer altogether. ☐

Keep your answers as brief as possible. Here's a similar question from a different text with a correct answer that is brief and to the point.

What is the colour of the football shirt James preferred?

Answer: red

3 Here are some answers which contain the right answer from the dialogues you heard. Make the answers really brief but make sure you still get the mark for being correct.

a) That'll be 600 euros altogether then. ....

b) About 700kg, the owner told me. ....

c) I suppose I had to make my own way for 10km – but 5km of that was across country.

....

d) It's just a shapeless blob – a great lump of glass and plastic.

....

Recognising numbers

Sometimes, you have to be able to recognise numbers to answer listening questions.

Make sure you know and can spell all the main number words.

1 Close your eyes and point to a position on the grid below. Then, write the number out in words in the space below. Do this at least five times; check your spellings in a dictionary.

8	10 000	1	19
13	40	3	2
12	14	15	6
4	17	7	18
60	5	30	20
11	70	50	10
90	100	1000	80
16	9	100 000	1 000 000

three ....

....

....

Top tip

In English, one billion is 1 000 000 millions. In American English, one billion is 1000 millions. As there is a potential for confusion, you should always write 'one billion' in words.

Practise writing and saying very long numbers, for example: 13 492 is *thirteen thousand, four hundred and ninety two*. When you have written this down and you are sure it is right, read it to a friend and see if they can write it down as a number.

2 Now complete this table:

1	first	5		9	
2	second	6		10	
3		7		11	
4		8		12	

Going further

Now for some extra practice, practise listening to numbers and writing them down. Listen to the recording of numbers that will be played to you.
4.3

3 a) The first time you hear the recording, write the numbers you hear as numerals in the spaces below. Listen carefully – sometimes there is more than one number.

1 2 ....   6 ....

2 ....   7 ....

3 ....   8 ....

4 ....   9 ....

5 ....   10 ....

b) On the second hearing, write them as words.

1 two ....   6 ....

2 ....   7 ....

3 ....   8 ....

4 ....   9 ....

5 ....   10 ....

4 Now listen to another recording and do the same again.
4.4

a) Write the numbers as numerals the first time you hear the recording.

1 1st ....   6 ....

2 ....   7 ....

3 ....   8 ....

4 ....   9 ....

5 ....   10 ....

b) The second time you hear the recording, write the numbers as words.

1 first ....   6 ....

2 ....   7 ....

3 ....   8 ....

4 ....   9 ....

5 ....   10 ....

3 Keeping the answers brief

5 You now have the chance to complete a full practice task.
Listen to the recording and answer the questions as directed.

4.5

For questions 1 to 6 you will hear a series of short sentences.

Answer each question on the line provided.

Your answers should be as brief as possible.

You will hear each item twice.

1: At what time will Aaron's mother pick him up from the airport?

....

2: How much does it cost for two tickets for the semi-final?

....

3: Why can't Irina go to the skate park?

....

4: How will Peter be able to spot Jen at the music festival?

....

5: What three camping items must Andreas bring for the trip?

....

....

....

6: What does the cake look like? Give two details:

....

....

4 Listening carefully for details

When you are doing a listening exercise where you have to fill in gaps in a form, always check that your answers make sense.

The question will help you, in that the spaces (the gaps on the form) will show you how long the answer should be. There will be a line of dots for each word that is missing. You should not try to squeeze a sentence into the space reserved for a single word. There is a strong chance that you might include wrong information and not get the mark!

This exercise will help you practise this skill.

1 Listen to the following interview about bees and then complete the details below:

Look at this form and complete the gaps in this form, using **one word or number** only for each gap.

Richard works as a ....

● Bees are used for producing ....

● Suffered from many ....

from the bees.

● Number of bees missing: ....

● Number of US states where same thing happened:

....

2 Now look at this answer and together decide where you would give one mark, and where you would give zero:

Richard works as a .....keeper............................

● Bees are used for producing ...honey.............................

● Suffered from many .put up with countless stings.

from the bees.

● Number of bees missing: ...1000 000 000...........................

● Number of US states where same thing happened:

twenty-four..............................

Further form-filling practice

3 Listen to an interview about a famous cycle race, the Tour de France, and then complete the details below.

The Tour de France

The Tour de France: a world-famous cycling race that tests people to the limit!

Where it takes place:

- Traditionally takes place in France, but some stages in nearby countries such as

  ....

- Goes through towns, cities and .... all over France.

- Finishes in Paris every year.

- Length of tour: ....

Teams and riders:

- About .... riders take part.

- Usually about 20–22 teams.

- .... riders in each team.

Winners:

Overall winner wears ....

The 'King of Mountains' wears ....

.... people have won more than once.

Conditions:

Temperatures can be .... and the landscape varies.

with .... and ....

5 Listening to monologues

The following task is a practice to help your prepare you for listening to monologues.

> **Top tip**
> • Listen very carefully to each speaker.
> • Think about what is different about what each speaker says.

1 You will hear six people talking about work and jobs. For each of Speakers 1 to 6, choose from the list A to G, which opinion each speaker expresses. Write the letter in the box. Use each letter only once. There is one extra letter which you do not need to use.

Speaker 1 ☐

Speaker 2 ☐

Speaker 3 ☐

Speaker 4 ☐

Speaker 5 ☐

Speaker 6 ☐

A: I am a creative person and like working for myself.

B: I love working and my life wouldn't be complete without a job.

C: I don't want to get promoted if it means telling other people what to do.

D: I am very confident and ambitious about the work I do.

E: I much prefer working outside to a job in an office.

F: I'd like to do a well-respected job, but I'm not sure I could handle the pressures.

G: I prefer having my independence and being able to relax.

Further practice: putting it all together

Part A

You will listen to a nutritionist giving a talk about chocolate, and whether it is good or bad for you. Listen to the talk and complete the notes in Part A. Write one or two words in each gap. You will hear the talk once.

Chocolate and the heart

Recent research suggests that moderate amounts of chocolate can prevent heart ....

There are chemicals which act as anti-oxidants. These can prevent damaging .... building up and polluting the body.

The reduction in risk of heart attack

Eating 100g of dark chocolate per day can reduce the risk by ....

Other benefits

Caffeine in chocolate can make you feel more alert.

Other chemicals can create a ....

Problems

The high amount of sugar in chocolate can cause ....

Part B

Now listen to a conversation between two students about whether chocolate is healthy or not, and complete the sentences in Part B. Write one or two words only in each gap. You will hear the conversation once.

New research:

Some researchers were concerned that testing people on chocolate wasn't very reliable.

The .... might be all in the mind.

So, they suggested it would be better to have imitation chocolate too and

use .... bars that looked like real ones to give people they tested.

Good advice

It is best to have chocolate .... a meal.

It is also a good idea to buy .... chocolate as it has less sugar in it.

It is very difficult to leave unfinished chocolate in the fridge.

So, buy .... as this means you will eat less, and it won't matter if you finish them.

---

6 Listening for multiple-choice answers

1 George, a student, is asking Susie Long, some questions about her circus act as part of a school radio programme. Read the questions and then listen to the conversation.

For each question choose the correct answer, **A**, **B** or **C** and put a tick [✓] in the appropriate box.

You will hear the talk twice.

a) What sort of events does Susie say she performs at?

   A: football matches ☐

   B: music festivals ☐

   C: birthday parties ☐

b) Why did Susie become a tightrope walker?

   A: Her family were circus performers. ☐

   B: She wasn't allowed to be a lion tamer. ☐

   C: She wasn't good at anything else. ☐

c) Who is showing signs of wanting to be a tightrope walker?

   A: Susie's younger brother ☐

   B: Susie's daughter ☐

   C: Susie's neighbour ☐

d) Susie doesn't use a bicycle in her act at the moment because:

   A: She wants to use a motorbike, like her father. ☐

   B: She prefers to do handstands. ☐

   C: She had a fall from a bicycle when she was practising. ☐

e) How was Susie cured of her fear?

   A: By practising and practising. ☐

   B: She read about a French high-wire artist. ☐

   C: She went to New York for help. ☐

f) How high was the wire Susie crossed in her show in Australia?

   A: 35 metres ☐

   B: 20 metres ☐

   C: 417 metres ☐

g) What does Susie do to prepare herself for a show?

   A: She listens to music. ☐

   B: She checks the towers on her own. ☐

   C: She does physical and breathing exercises. ☐

h) What new act is Susie working on at the moment?

   A: diving from a high platform ☐

   B: swaying on a 25-metre pole ☐

   C: carrying her daughter on her shoulders ☐

William Collins's dream of knowledge for all began with the publication of his first book in 1819. A self-educated mill worker, he not only enriched millions of lives but also founded a flourishing publishing house. Today, staying true to this spirit, Collins books are packed with inspiration, innovation and practical expertise. They place you at the centre of a world of possibility and give you exactly what you need to explore it.

Collins. Freedom to teach.

Published by Collins Education
An imprint of HarperCollins*Publishers*
77–85 Fulham Palace Road
London W6 8JB

Browse the complete Collins Education catalogue at www.collinseducation.com

© HarperCollins*Publishers* Limited 2013
10 9 8 7 6 5 4 3 2

ISBN 978 0 00 745689 5

® IGCSE is the registered trademark of Cambridge International Examinations.

British Library Cataloguing in Publication Data.
A Catalogue record for this publication is available from the British Library.

Commissioned by Andrew Campbell
Project managed by Jo Kemp
Copyediting by Lucy Hobbs
Design by JPD
Page design by Graham Brasnett, Cambridge
Cover design by Paul Manning
Picture research by Stephen Haskins and Grace Glendinning

With thanks to our reviewers: Catherine Errigton, Italy; Dean Roberts, UK; Rohan Roberts, UAE; Alan Schmidt, Czech Republic; Naghma Shaikh, India

Acknowledgements
The publishers gratefully acknowledge the permission granted to reproduce the copyright material in this book. While every effort has been made to trace and contact copyright holders, where this has not been possible the publishers will be pleased to make the necessary arrangements at the first opportunity.

Pp 6–7 from http://www.basketball-camp-spain.com/Basketball-Camp-Spain-Overview. html; pp 12, 13 and 15 from *Horse and Hound* magazine, © Horse & Hound/IPC+ Syndication; p 78 from http://www.betterhealth.vic.gov.au/bhcv2/bhcarticles.nsf/pages/ Fear_of_the_dark_children

The publisher would like to thank the following for permission to reproduce pictures in these pages (t = top, b = bottom, c = centre, l = left, r = right):
p 6 dotshock/Shutterstock, pp 12 & 13 Gavriel Jecan/Getty Images, pp 12b Uwe Halstenbach/iStockphoto, p 17 Kablonk/SuperStock, p 30 solarseven/Shutterstock, p 47c Andi Berger/Shutterstock, p 47l winhorse/iStockphoto, p 47r Khafizov Ivan Harisovich/Shutterstock, p 53 Photononstop/SuperStock, p 68 Thomas Barrat/ Shutterstock, p 74 Fotosearch/SuperStock, p 75 Studio MARMILADE/Shutterstock, p 89t dirkr/Shutterstock, p89c Skylines/Shutterstock, p 89b Fer Gregory/Shutterstock, p 99 age fotostock/SuperStock, p 100 John Kershner/Shutterstock.

Audio tracks in section 4
4.1 (p 91); 4.2 (p 93); 4.3 (p 97); 4.4 (p 97); 4.5 (p 98); 4.6 (p 99); 4.7 (p 100); 4.8 (p 101); 4.9 (p 102); 4.10 (p 102); 4.11 (p 103)